The Dream Child

The Dream Child

Meghan Stewart

iUniverse, Inc.
New York Lincoln Shanghai

The Dream Child

iUniverse, Inc.

For information address:
iUniverse, Inc.
2021 Pine Lake Road, Suite 100
Lincoln, NE 68512
www.iuniverse.com

ISBN: 0-595-28188-5

Printed in the United States of America

Dedicated to:

TRACY
AND ALL
OTHER PARENTS
WHO SUFFER DEEPLY
BECAUSE
THEY
LOVE DEEPLY
AND TO
NAOMI JOY TAYLOR,
MY
DREAM CHILD

Contents

Taylor Family Members ix

Part I

March, 1993 3

June 1981 5

September, 1981 10

Christmas, 1981 15

January, 1982—A New Year 18

February, 1982 23

Spring ~ 1982 29

Part II

Warfare? 39

The Nightmare 46

Part III

School Days ~ Kindergarten 87

1st Grade ~ The Elf 91

2nd Grade—Farewell to the Elf! 96

Part IV

Changes 101

Reconciliation 108

May, 1990 112

April 1992 119

The Investigation 123

Again 127

And Again 135

March 25, 1996—A Letter of Love 145

August, 1997—A Final Letter 148

Epilogue 151

Taylor Family Members

Adam and Maggie—Foster/adoptive parents

Jason—First son—Caucasian—Brought into the family at five days of age—Picked up from the hospital where he was born

Naomi Joy—First daughter—Asian—Brought into family from Korea—Lived with birth mother, followed by an orphanage, to a foster home, and finally to the home of Adam and Maggie at six months of age—later diagnosed as Reactive Attachment Disorder

Troy and Tammi—Foster/adopt siblings—black—four and two years of age—removed from a foster home as an emergency placement—remained with the Taylor family for nine months

Paul and Ruth—Foster/adopt siblings—Caucasian—Paul came at three years of age—this was his fourteenth move—later diagnosed as Reactive Attachment Disorder and Fetal Alcohol Effect; Ruth came at twenty-three months of age—this was her eighth move—later diagnosed as mild Attachment Disorder, Attention Deficit/Hyperactive Disorder and Fetal Alcohol Effect

Tori—Foster/adopt girl—Asian—Brought into the family at three days of age—Picked up from the hospital where she was born

Note that all names have been changed

PART I

March, 1993

The call came in the middle of the afternoon. "Good afternoon, Maggie here!" Maggie, the mother of two adopted children, Naomi, twelve years old and Jason, fourteen, answered with the greeting that remained the same day after day, week after week, month after month. Most people liked it and responded with cheerfulness. She had reason to be cheerful. In a matter of days, she and her husband, Adam, would be finalizing the adoption of three more children. Paul, four years old, and his sister, Ruth, now two, in addition to baby Tori, all of six months old would soon be permanent members of their little family. The woman on the other end of the line, however, didn't respond with any lift in her voice.

"Hello, Maggie. This is Candy." Her friend engaged Maggie in some small talk before getting to the real issue.

"I thought you would want to know what Naomi is telling people. I got it from my daughter, and it's all over the school."

Maggie had a sinking feeling in the pit of her stomach. What could it be now? It seemed like things were going fairly well—and the adoption was coming up in just one week. "Okay, Candy, tell me. I think I'm ready."

"Naomi told the other girls at school that the mark on her face is from being slapped—by you."

"Oh no. What mark on her face? She didn't have any marks on her face when she left for school this morning!"

"Well," returned Candy, "there are marks now. And she says that you did it. I just wanted to let you know…And see if there's anything I can do. Do you need help or anything? Are the children giving you a bad time? I can understand frustration, maybe even to pushing Ruth down the stairs, but…"

Maggie was appalled. "*What? What did you say about Ruth?*"

"Naomi said, well, that you pushed Ruth down the stairs, and now she is afraid to go down them at all…I was worried…"

"Candy, you have known me for years. You know I would not hurt my little girl! Push her down the stairs?! Candy, I have never…"

"There's more, Maggie. Does little Tori have a burn on her hand?"

Maggie sat down hard in the nearby chair. "Oh, my God. Oh, my God."

"Maggie, are you all right?"

Maggie's voice was barely audible. She whispered, "Yes, but it was an accident. Jason set her right next to a hot casserole dish on the table. He didn't mean to see her hurt. It was only an accident. He wouldn't hurt Tori for the world!"

Candy's voice was quiet. "Naomi didn't say anything about Jason, Maggie."

Understanding slowly seeped into every part of Maggie's being. "Why would she do this? Why would she say these things? Surely no one would believe this!"

"I'm afraid a lot of people believe it, Maggie. I don't know how far it has gone—how far it will go. But I thought you should know." There weren't many words of comfort Candy could offer—and after hearing Maggie's denial, she still wasn't convinced Naomi's allegations were false. People can do some horrible things under stress and Naomi sounded so convincing. But, Candy had known Maggie a long time, and Maggie didn't seem the sort—although she didn't know for sure what "the sort" was. They talked a bit longer, until Candy had to go.

Maggie stayed in the chair for a long time, tears running down her face. She tried so hard to love this child. Naomi, why do you do these things? How much pain will you inflict? Where will it end? Who has heard? Have my other friends heard this—and do they believe it? Why would they even think I could...Sobs broke out....I could burn my own baby? Burn her?! Never! And push little Ruth down the stairs? Oh my God, help me! What will I say to Naomi? How can I respond? It hurts, oh it hurts, it hurts...Rocking back and forth, hugging her arms close, Maggie sat and cried.

Jason and Naomi were out with Maggie's husband, Adam, for awhile. Tori and Ruth were both sleeping in the room they shared. Paul, almost five years old now, was in his room and quiet for the time being. Maggie thought—somehow she would need to respond to Naomi when she got home. She and Jason were playing in the same band, so they would return together soon. What will I say? How can I deal with this? I don't know how to talk to Naomi about this. We've had a hard time since she came—but how do I take care of this situation? Maggie wished there was someone she could talk to about this, but who would really understand? Even Adam had difficulty seeing how hurtful Naomi's actions were. How would he react? The tears kept coming, but there seemed to be no answers.

Finally, Maggie was able to stop crying and remembered that day, the first time she had heard of this beautiful baby girl, who Maggie dreamed would grow up to become a beautiful young lady. How could she do such a terrible thing?

June 1981

Maggie held the receiver of the telephone tightly. She could hardly believe her ears. Finally, they would be adding to their family! It was so hard to believe because they had been searching out possibilities since little Jason was only a year old. It took four years to get him, and who could say how long it would be before they could find a second child?

Adam and Maggie had come to terms with the thought of raising Jason as an only child. They knew they were truly blessed to have him! How long they waited for their precious son. How much they wanted a baby. So many others carried little ones in their arms, especially there in Utah. It had been bad enough in Colorado, but in Utah, it seemed everyone had at least one baby in his arms. Well, maybe not everyone, but a lot of them. Large families were the norm in the area, a result of religious beliefs in the community. How many people didn't even want their babies? Adam and Maggie so desperately wanted a child; yet were unable to conceive because of medical problems. When they got little Jason, it was such a miracle! Maggie remembered the day the agency called as if it were just yesterday.

Their first baby was due the eighth of December. Each day seemed to stretch into eternity as Maggie waited for the phone to ring. Often someone would call, asking if the baby had yet been born. This intensified Maggie's frustration. When the baby arrived, she would see to it that the whole world knew it! She'd announce it to everyone she knew! Besides, if she was on the phone with a well-meaning friend when the all-important call finally came, she'd miss it!

It was late afternoon on December twenty-ninth when the phone rang. Maggie answered it as always, "Good afternoon, Maggie here." The voice on the other end said, "It's a boy!" Of course, she knew immediately what he meant. Maggie began to sob, "A boy, a boy, we got a boy!" She became totally overwhelmed by emotion. She wanted a boy so badly, but just knew down deep that it would be a girl for Adam! Oh, how he wanted a daughter! His dream has always been to have his own little girl. But no, at long last, God had granted the desire of her heart and given her a boy! She had wanted her first child, perhaps only child, to be a boy! How she rejoiced that her prayer was answered!

Maggie's crying awakened her sleeping husband. Adam worked nights then, and slept during the day; but not so soundly that he could sleep through Maggie's excitement. He got up and took the phone. It was obvious that Maggie couldn't get any of the other information. He got some details—time of birth, weight, length. He forgot to ask if he had any hair. Maggie wanted to know if the baby had blond hair, like Adam's. The truly important information, however, was that they could fly out to pick their new son up any time.

Their pastor, who owned a small airplane, was to fly the couple to Arkansas to pick up the baby. He was almost as exhilarated as the new parents were. Yet, the pastor had church obligations to be met that delayed the trip. Those days of waiting were agony for both Adam and Maggie. Now that they knew about their baby, Maggie ached to hold him!

It was five days before Pastor, Adam and Maggie were able to fly out to Arkansas to pick up Jason. Even when they arrived at the hospital, they had to wait. It was the hospital policy that the adoptive parents could not enter the hospital where the new baby was born. "Adoption" automatically meant "closed adoption". To maintain the anonymity of the birth parent(s), there was to be no "accidental" contact. Therefore, Adam and Maggie had to wait in the van while until the hospital personnel brought the baby out to them.

When Maggie held Jason in her arms for the first time, she had never experienced anything like it. Many times she had held other babies. But this baby was different. She savored the joy of holding her very own baby. Maggie was amazed at the sense of awe she felt as she gazed down into his face. He was a big boy—nine pounds and eleven ounces. He did have hair—not much—but hair none-the-less, and it was reddish blond, like Adam's. He had blue eyes, too. Maggie laughed out loud—she had wanted a blond-haired, blue eyed little boy, a child that looked like her husband. Perhaps if he looked like Adam, father and son would somehow be more deeply bonded. This child was perfect—ten toes, ten fingers, a darling little nose, and he did look remarkably like his adoptive father! So precious.

When Maggie and Adam got little Jason to the hotel, the first thing they did was to strip him naked, lay him on the bed and admire every inch of him. Oh, how precious, how innocent, how exquisite. And he was theirs! How long did they stand and admire him? After awhile, they dressed him, fed him, and cuddled him…

They had often talked about their family. Maggie and Adam agreed that they wanted at least six children. After Jason turned one, they began their search for another child. They tried several organizations, but when the waiting lists were so long, they were discouraged and found all the good reasons to raise an "only child". Then they found an organization, willing to work with this little family of three, and find a child in Korea for them, a little girl. It took two years. Jason was three years old when Maggie finally held the phone and heard those long awaited words, "I am holding a picture of a three month old baby girl. I thought you might be interested…"

Interested! Maggie couldn't wait to hear more. This beautiful infant had lots of black hair, perfect little almond shaped black eyes, and a birthmark on her left big toe! It was this birthmark that placed the babe in the category of "special needs". Adam and Maggie had told the agency that they were open to the placement of a child with certain disabilities, specifically deafness. Maggie loved her work with deaf children and felt that her experience with "her" young ones could be an asset.

"Of course," assured the caseworker, "this will need to be monitored on a regular basis as it may well be a melanoma that would need to be surgically removed. We will include a picture of it in the packet we send, should you be interested in following up on this possibility…"[1]

Other than that birthmark, the child was a perfect, Korean baby girl. Interested?! Could there be any question—any doubt at all?!

Maggie rejoiced! She picked up Jason and danced around the kitchen with him, saying, "Jason, they found her! They found your little sister!" He laughed and cried and sang along with his mother. They couldn't wait to call Daddy! He wanted a baby girl so much! Maggie had to rush next door to tell Carrie. Carrie's little girl, Kirsten, and Jason were only two months apart. Carrie's second little girl, Marti, and this new baby were even closer in age! Maggie couldn't help looking at little Marti and imagining what her own daughter would be like. Her daughter! Maggie relished the sound of it. Her very own daughter!

Of course, they were advised, there was lots of red tape, paper work, fees, etc. to work through. But how could it not be worth it?! Anything for their own little girl would certainly be "worth it"! Adam had already chosen her name. Maggie chose Jason's, so Adam got to choose his new daughter's name. It would be Naomi Joy. Naomi means "pleasant". They already knew she would be pleasant to look upon! Joy is for the joy they had this day. Naomi Joy. It was an ideal name.

The fees were simply incredible, and the airfare would be due now! Maggie reflected on the amazing way the money had been coming in. Of course, they had

---

1.   Interestingly enough, the birthmark gradually faded away, never causing a problem.

raised and saved some of it while waiting; but the rest was all a product of many miracles. Like the day Maggie and Jason had gone to the mailbox and found two checks inside. Together they amounted to a grand total of $900! Maggie's younger sister, as well as the rest of her family, were excited about the coming baby and shared the story with their churches. Responding in love, one of the congregations sent a check. The second was from an air force friend who had been transferred to England. He was gone a long time ~ but kept in touch. He "just had this extra money" and sent it!

Then there was the family in their own church that was moving out of state. One day they called and told Maggie that they had something they didn't want to move. Would Maggie and Adam consider taking it? Well, it certainly depended on what it was, and how big it was. It was big alright ~ it was their savings account! Unbelievable!

Money came from everywhere, sometime anonymously and sometimes from the hand of a friend or group. But few of them touched their hearts as much as the gift from young Kirk. He was the son of one of the elders at their little church. Kirk was saving newspapers, which he turned in for cash at the recycling center. He had quite a pile in his dad's garage. He planned to use the money for a special project of his own. Yet, when he sold those newspapers, he gave the entire amount to Maggie and Adam for the baby. Compared to some of the other gifts, the amount was small, but Maggie and Adam thought it might just be one of the biggest!

◆   ◆   ◆

Maggie vividly remembered that day, hearing for the first time of their little girl. She continued to sit, and remember the days that followed—the funny times, the hard times. It had been so difficult to continue on as Naomi Joy grew, not knowing from one day to the next what she would do. Who would call next, what would be broken, or stolen?

Time was short, Naomi Joy, Jason and Adam would soon be home…Maggie's mind wandered, to that very first time she had seen little Naomi Joy…

There was so much they hadn't been told, didn't know. They were able to piece some things together…If only they had known. If only someone had told them…

Naomi Joy[2] was born in Korea at a time and in a place known only by her birth mother. Her mother knew that there was little hope for this tiny baby in her native country, and had her placed in an orphanage. She was soon moved from there to a foster home, in anticipation of a move to the United States of America—a place of hope, a place where this little one would have a future impossible for her in Korea. Many things happened to Naomi Joy during those brief months, things unspoken and unrecorded, things hidden that they might never be revealed, except perhaps by the child's behavior as she matured. So it was that she arrived in America at the age of six months, her fourth home in her short life.

Naomi Joy arrived in Denver, CO. on a beautiful September morning. She was ill. Ear infections had been torturing her for all of her life, and had never been treated. She was sedated for the trip over the ocean, and as the medication wore off, her pain became intolerable. Naomi Joy cried throughout the afternoon and most of the night. So began her life in her new country...

Could it have been just coincidence that Maggie happened to be vacationing in Denver with family, when word arrived that Naomi Joy would be flown into the Denver airport in just two more days? Of course, as soon as he heard the great news, Adam made no delay in arranging a flight to meet Maggie in Denver. He called Maggie to let her know that he would be joining her and their son, so that all three of them could meet Naomi Joy as a family. There had been so much red tape, taking three months to get everything in order before their new daughter could join them. She was no longer just three months old, but six! Maggie spent hours making her beautiful dresses and shopping for just the right things. The crib was set up, diapers in the diaper stacker, the diaper bag all packed just waiting for this day!

Adam arrived the next day. Jason was excited to see his Daddy and raced into his waiting arms. "Your sister is coming tomorrow, Jason! Remember the name we picked out for her?"

"Oh, yes, Daddy! Naomi Joy, because she is a joy, and she will be a pleasant little sister!"

Daddy laughed and you could see the happiness in his eyes, as he listened to his son and thought of the beautiful little girl he had waited for so long. Soon he would hold her in his arms.

---

2.   Born to a Korean name, which means "Beautiful" and "wise", changed by her adoptive parents to "Naomi Joy".

September, 1981

The telephone rang. The worker at the agency said that Naomi Joy's airplane from Korea was delayed. Maggie was far too excited to wait. She and her mother-in-law, Loreen, would go shopping and pick up a couple of cute little dresses, or shoes, or something! Adam could stay in the home with his dad and Jason to wait for the worker to call back.

Loreen and Maggie had a wonderful time together preparing for the arrival of Naomi Joy. They found all kinds of baby things, but finally settled on a red dress, tights and tiny shoes. When they found the shoes, Maggie laughed. She reminded Loreen of their conversation in which Maggie had shared that Naomi Joy had a "special need" (other than being a minority!). They had laughed together about the small birthmark on her big toe when Loreen said, "Well, when we go to the beach, we'll have to draw petals around it and pretend it's a flower tattoo!".

When they arrived back at Loreen's house, Adam met them at the door with a surprise. Jason was jumping up and down, trying to be the first to tell them the news. While Loreen and Maggie were out, the agency called and said, not only had the plane arrived on time, they had gone and picked up Naomi Joy! She was waiting at the agency for Adam and Maggie to come get her! So it was that, not Maggie and Adam went together to meet Naomi Joy; but rather <u>Jason</u> and Adam had the privilege!

Maggie drank in every detail as she gazed into the face of <u>her</u> little "China doll". Naomi Joy had dark almond shaped eyes. She had black, flyaway hair, and lots of it! The baby had ten perfect fingers. Her tiny feet looked fine to Maggie. Maggie wondered what the nonsense was all about when the agency was so concerned about a birthmark. Oh, yes, there it was—the tiny birthmark, maybe even too small to paint petals around it! Naomi Joy looked so perfect. Maggie held out her arms and Adam gently placed the six-month-old in them for the first time. A gentle smile played on Maggie's lips as she looked down, greeting that beautiful, finely chiseled face. Yes, Naomi Joy was indeed a name befitting this child of her dreams—her Dream Child! Adam smiled, too. He was delighted that <u>his</u> "little princess" had finally arrived!

Naomi Joy was calm and quiet for awhile, her eyes almost seeming unfocused. Of course, she was only six months old, thought Maggie; but she should be able to focus a little better. Then Naomi Joy began to cry. As the evening wore on, Naomi Joy cried more and more, louder and louder, until she was screaming. After a very noisy dinner and some playtime for Jason, he was sent to bed. Eventually Adam went to bed as well, as did Adam's father. Only Loreen and Maggie stayed up with the screaming baby. Loreen suggested that Maggie lay down for a bit and rest, while she tried to rock the baby to sleep. Maggie had already tried everything she could think of to calm the baby—now, hopefully, Loreen could help. She had far more experience after raising her own five children!

But Naomi Joy was inconsolable. All that night, she screamed, occasionally quieting to a sad little whimper, then escalating again. Loreen and Maggie traded off throughout the night, one trying to rest, and the other rocking and rocking and rocking that poor little baby. By early morning, Naomi Joy's body was limp, exhausted from the hours of crying. Even as she finally slept, she would often whimper as she shifted position, sometimes crying out pitifully, then dozing off for a few more minutes. Adam and Maggie agreed that the first thing they would do when they arrived home with Jason and Naomi Joy would be to take the baby to the doctor.

At the pediatrician's office, a number of things became apparent. Naomi Joy had been drugged for the trip to the United States. Her ears were so full of infection; she could not have flown otherwise. It was evident that she had suffered from this infection since shortly after birth—and had never been treated! There was so much scar tissue the doctor had no idea how this child could hear at all! In addition, Naomi Joy had a skin condition—dermatitis the doctor called it. It was impossible to find a clear spot on the baby's body. Sores appeared red and rashy to seeping and running. Between the ear infections and the dermatitis, her pain was terrible. This child, most likely, had not lived a single day of her life without pain. It appeared that she had grown accustomed to it. It would take two years before her ears and skin healed.

Those first few months were a nightmare. Maggie had few happy memories of that time. There was just screaming, and screaming and more screaming. She and Adam quickly established a routine. Maggie would hold Naomi Joy for two hours, rocking her, talking to her, trying to play, feeding her, even backpacking her around, but her crying was relentless. She even cried when she ate—because she would fill up both hands with her finger foods, and stuff her mouth so full she was unable to chew! This was incredibly frustrating for her, so she would cry, even more upset as food dribbled out of her mouth. Maggie and Adam tried giving her smaller amounts, only spoon foods, very soft foods, but nothing worked. She just had to have her hands and mouth full.

After that two hours, Maggie sat on the floor, holding Naomi Joy, and try to play with Jason—as Naomi Joy cried. Jason enjoyed the play, and he showed great patience with his new sister. He couldn't understand why she kept crying, but he knew something was wrong. He would try handing her toys, and slowly she began to respond. He learned to coax a smile out of her; sometimes she would actually laugh for him.

Then Maggie put Naomi Joy in her crib, shut the door and tried to accomplish something around the house. She and Jason would do the dishes, wash laundry, can produce from the garden, sit and talk or watch Sesame Street together. Maggie loved watching the program with Jason. Ever since he turned one year old, he considered himself much too old and mature to be held and cuddled anymore. But, if "his" show was on, he would snuggle up in the bean bag chair with his mommy. They would watch and laugh together. Then the routine began again, two hours holding, two hours holding and playing with Jason, and then two hours of time alone or with Jason, all the while enduring Naomi Joy's cries.

One afternoon, as Maggie, Naomi Joy and Jason sat playing, the doorbell rang. Maggie picked up the baby, and with Jason following after, they went to answer the door. A stranger stood there staring at the trio. "I heard the screaming as I was walking down the street, and thought I'd stop to see if something was wrong…"

Maggie looked at the woman. No, she didn't recognize her. Even though all the doors and windows were closed against the cool autumn weather, this woman had heard Naomi Joy crying. Maggie hoped she didn't look or sound as haggard as she was when she answered, "No, we are fine. The baby is just upset. She'll be fine in a bit, after her lunch." Maggie was lying. Of course, Naomi Joy wouldn't be better after her lunch. They had just finished lunch and she was no better. But she wanted this woman to leave them alone. When she left, Maggie put Naomi Joy in the crib, shut the door, turned on the TV for Jason, and went into her own room to cry. Again. No matter what she did, how hard she tried; she could not calm this baby. They both cried and cried and cried. Maybe Maggie was just a lousy mom. Yet, Jason had never been so inconsolable. What could be wrong? Why was she failing so miserably? What could she do? Naomi Joy was crying sixteen hours a day, every day, and often through the night. Maggie couldn't get away from it, couldn't stop it, couldn't sleep, and often couldn't eat. It was so hard. Now the hurtful situation was magnified by this well meaning stranger's intrusion.

One morning, the noise from the children's bedroom seemed unusually loud. Maggie went to the bedroom Jason and Naomi Joy were sharing. As she peeked in, there was Naomi Joy, standing in her crib, gripping the side and leaning as far over it as she could manage, eyes on her brother, screaming at him as if to say, "JASON, WAKE UP! PLAY WITH ME!" Yet, there in his little bed, lay Jason, peacefully sleeping, totally oblivious to the noise. Maggie smiled to herself. He had learned to sleep through it all. What a remarkable child.

Maggie remembered when Jason had first come home and seemed to sleep so much. She wanted him to wake up so she could play with him, but she knew better than to wake up a peacefully sleeping baby. Occasionally, she vacuumed right under his crib, and he still slept peacefully. Adam laughed at her. He said that the only reason she wanted children was so she could have someone to play with! He was probably right—and play she did! What fun they had together.

Maggie went in and picked up Naomi Joy. "Silly baby. It looks like even the 'Scream Machine' can't wake up that big brother. Might as well give up. I've tried it too—and once he's asleep, he stays that way 'til he's ready to get up. How about some breakfast, Pumpkin?" Maggie laughed and got clothes to dress the baby. Feeling content, she chose something really cute. Many mornings, she didn't care what the child wore. Sometimes she was able to laugh at the little things. But it would be nice if she could get a good night's sleep.

The days dragged by. Occasionally, they could get out and walk, go to the park, or go shopping. Maggie liked taking the children out. It was one of the rare times Naomi Joy seemed to be happy. She would look around with such interest, soaking in everything. People looked at that beautiful Asian child and were drawn to her beauty. Maggie loved the attention Naomi Joy got and how people wanted to talk about her. They would ask how old she was and where she was from.

One day, while out shopping with, Jason and Naomi Joy, Maggie and Adam were talking as they waited in the line to check out. They were preparing for Christmas and were excited about the upcoming celebration. Suddenly, the man just behind them gasped in surprise. Adam and Maggie quickly turned around to see what had happened.

The gentleman looked embarrassed. "Oh, I was just so surprised when your baby in the cart moved. I thought she was a doll!"

Adam and Maggie laughed as they looked at their beautiful daughter. Naomi Joy smiled. "Yes, she is so pretty, she does look like a doll, doesn't she?!" Maggie thought so beautiful on the outside, so broken on the inside.

"Mommy! Mommy, please come quick!" It was Jason, in the bedroom. Something was wrong. Maggie to see Jason standing beside the crib, obviously shaken. "Look, Mommy. I wanted to play with Naomi, but look!"

Naomi Joy was asleep, but blood was all over her sheets, blankets and nightie. Maggie gasped. She quickly slid the side of the crib down as she instructed Jason to go get a nice warm wash cloth. He needed something to do to distract him. Maggie pulled up the nightie. During the night, Naomi Joy had scratched her legs viciously from the ankle to the top of her thigh. Here was something that a bath couldn't fix.

It wasn't the first time something like this had happened. Since they first brought her home, Naomi Joy would scratch at her ears until they bled. It was the chronic ear infections, Maggie thought. They put little bonnets on her every night before bed so she couldn't get to her ears. It worked, but now she was scratching her legs until they bled, too. Maggie and Jason got her into a bath. After Maggie dressed her daughter; she left Naomi Joy and Jason playing while she washed the soiled bedclothes.

Maggie went to the sewing machine. She made mittens to match each nightie. Maggie left a hole for the baby's thumb so she could still grasp and hold things. But Naomi Joy's little fingernails would be covered. Maggie would talk to the doctor again. She sighed deeply, suspecting he would have the same answer as always. "It should pass. Just be patient. Just keep loving her. Just keep loving her. Just keep loving her."

Christmas, 1981

Maggie had been convinced that within three months, just three months, things would be better. Surely, this living hell would end by then. No baby could continue to live in such torment for any longer than that! Maggie tried so hard to help Naomi Joy; yet nothing seemed to make any difference for the unhappy infant. There *had* been moments of fun with Naomi Joy and Jason, but Christmas this year was so difficult. It should have been such a happy time, but Maggie was so tired, so very tired…

The mittens did look kind of cute with all of little Naomi Joy's nighties, but it did not stop the scratching problem. If she worked at it long enough, Naomi Joy could even get those off and scratched again until she drew blood. Thank God it was never as bad as it was that awful day when Jason had looked upon his new little sister with such horror, but the screaming did not stop. She wasn't crying constantly. She was down from twenty hours a day to between nine and fifteen. At night was the worst—crying and crying, not to be consoled. Maggie couldn't remember the last time she had a full night's sleep. For sure, it was more than three months ago! She was just so tired. So very, very tired.

Maggie did take some pleasure in the bit of sewing she could do. She made an adorable little sweatsuit for Jason. Of course it was in the colors of the Steelers! They had to make sure to come home from church each Sunday in time to watch the football game of the day, *especially* if it was the Steelers playing. Not for Adam—or even for Maggie. No, it was Jason's passion. Where does such interest come from? Neither Adam nor Maggie had ever been interested in sports of any kind yet little Jason was well coordinated and absolutely loved football. He was so cute at the age of two, learning to "hike" that football! Now, at four, he was even more fascinated by the sport. She knew that, when he knelt by the Christmas tree, and pulled out this gift; he'd absolutely love the sweatsuit. She could hardly wait to watch him open it; not to mention put it on! She couldn't wait to see him in it!

She made a beautiful, lacy little dress for Naomi Joy. It had ribbons and lace and was so cute! She even bought fancy tights to go with it. One of the greatest things about Naomi Joy was her attractiveness, and dressing her up to take her out was something Maggie could really enjoy! This one was the cutest outfit she ever made for her tiny daughter.

Naomi Joy had learned to sit up, but refused to crawl. There was only one way for her to get around ~ and that was to be carried! Left on the floor, Naomi Joy would cry and cry. Pick her up and she was alert and taking everything around her in. Maggie wished there was a way to do nothing all day but carry Naomi Joy around ~ Naomi Joy would be happy then. But Naomi Joy was becoming heavy enough that it was difficult for Maggie to carry her around even in the backpack ~ which Naomi Joy didn't like anyway. It seemed that Naomi Joy's motto was "Carry me or watch me cry"!

Christmas dawned—a beautiful, Utah, winter morning. Jason was eagerly awaiting release from his bedroom. He knew that there would be surprises under the tree and in his stocking, so carefully hung the night before after Daddy read the Christmas story from the Bible. He was well aware, on this, his fourth Christmas, that he must wait here at the door until Mommy came to tell him "Merry Christmas"! It was so difficult to wait, but he had amused himself telling Naomi Joy about Christmas and all that it meant. Naomi Joy seemed to understand him, and to share his enthusiasm. When Maggie came to the door, two children welcomed her with smiles, their eyes sparkling with anticipation.

"Daddy is waiting for you! He has the camera ready, and there are some surprises in the living room! Are you ready?" Foolish question, of course, but Maggie was relishing this precious moment.

"Yes, yes, yes!" exclaimed Jason, jumping up and down. Naomi Joy watched, grasped the railing of her crib and joined in, bouncing in her crib, squealing!

Naomi Joy loved Christmas! Adam took lots of pictures! There was a beautiful new dress for her (and tights), lots of pretty paper ribbon and bows to play with, and plenty to eat! Next to the food, the most wonderful thing Naomi Joy found was the kitty. When it was wound up, it would noisily wander through the room, bouncing off of walls and furniture. Naomi Joy felt she just must catch it and before she realized, she was actually crawling after it! Adam and Maggie rejoiced together as they watched nine month old Naomi chase that toy around the house! She would laugh and move more quickly than Adam and Maggie imagined! Jason watched, clapped, encouraged his sister, and rewound that toy until Adam and Maggie wondered if it would last the full day!

At bedtime, when Maggie changed Naomi Joy into her nightie, there on the baby's legs was the exact pattern of the lacy tights that had looked so adorable. Maggie sighed. Naomi Joy had that awful rash all over her body and when anyone touched her, an imprint clearly showed. It was such an odd thing. While playing, if anyone drew a letter on her back, it was visible on her skin for a long time. When food came in contact with her face while she ate, it left painful welts. Maggie took a bit of the ointment the doctor had prescribed for the rash and rubbed it gently into Naomi Joy's legs. Poor thing, the itch must have been awful. No wonder she scratched and scratched all night long. There wasn't a patch of clear skin on her. She continued to be covered with this rash from head to foot. Nothing really helped. She broke out, scratched, and ended up with open, seeping sores all over her little body. Even this Christmas night would be yet another sleepless vigil.

January, 1982—A New Year

Maggie could feel it happening. It was like standing at the edge of a cliff. She could look down, down, down, feel herself falling, but she could do nothing to stop it. She was losing her grip on life itself. The crying and crying and crying, it just never stopped. "Oh, God, how can I go on? Please help me. Please don't let me go crazy!" She looked at the glass in her hand. She used to drink and party. Now she was drinking and just trying to survive. She could hear Naomi Joy crying even as she swallowed the contents of the glass and closed her eyes. Maybe it would dull her pain.

Maggie became filled with self-doubt. Nothing she did helped Naomi Joy. How could she be such a rotten mother? It hadn't been like this with Jason. He was such an easy baby to care for. He only cried when he was hungry or dirty. Change the baby, feed him, and he was a smiling, happy little boy. But now, she couldn't do _anything_ right. No matter what she did, the baby cried. Maybe one more shot, she thought and filled her glass again. The smell of the alcohol rose to her nostrils and her hand shook as she lifted it to her lips. She prayed. "God, please, help me…"

Adam was becoming more and more concerned. His little princess was such a sweetie. He would come home and hold the baby, rock her, play with her, and Naomi Joy would smile! Maggie wondered why Adam hadn't noticed that Naomi Joy seemed to be smirking, not smiling. Maggie felt that the little one was smirking at her, ridiculing her. Was she trying to say, "Daddy's mine now!"? Adam could not understand what was going on. Maggie was obviously hurting, tired, hating life. But why? Naomi Joy was cute; Jason was so active and busy. Life was good. "So what was going on? What was happening when I am gone?", thought Adam. "Is Maggie going to be okay?" He suspected she was drinking again. She had been quite a partier when he met her, when she was in college. But, since they had gotten married, she only drank occasionally, socially. Maybe he should talk with the Pastor. He could help get a handle on this. It sure couldn't hurt!

18

◆   ◆   ◆

Monday again. The weekends were a little bit easier, with Adam home. He could get Naomi Joy to smile, even to laugh. In fact, this was the best time. They went to church together. Of course Maggie had to stay in the nursery since Naomi Joy refused to stay without screaming, and all the workers wanted Maggie there, or Naomi Joy to leave. At least there were other adults to talk to, and other children to watch. Naomi Joy would play happily with them as Maggie sat nearby. Saturday and Sunday afternoons (after the football game!) the family would play together, and those were happier times. Naomi Joy still couldn't sleep through the night, but Adam slept through the noise. Maggie couldn't, but she managed to sleep a little during the day as Adam cared the children. But now it was Monday, Adam was at work, and while the children were "napping" (Jason was napping anyway…), Maggie got out her own bottle and glass. Suddenly the phone rang.

"Hello," Maggie answered.

"Good afternoon, Maggie. This is Daniel. What are you doing?"

Ahhh, Pastor Daniel. Of all people. Maggie used to care what other people thought about her. Now she thought to herself, "Who cares? What difference does it make what he thinks of me? It doesn't matter anyway." Maggie laughed before she answered. "I am sitting here, getting drunker than a skunk. How about you—what are you doing?"

Pastor Daniel did not miss a beat. "I want you to pour out that drink. I am on my way over. If you still have it when I get there, I am going to beat the hell out of you. Then I will hold you, and remind you how precious you are to the Lord and the people around you."

Maggie could not believe her ears. This was not how a pastor was supposed to talk! Of course, Pastor Daniel wasn't your run of the mill pastor. He'd seen it all. He understood what life is like in the real world, and how to help people face it. And now, he was on his way over. Maggie poured the rest of the bottle down the drain.

◆   ◆   ◆

Maggie, Adam and Pastor Daniel put together a plan to help Maggie cope with little Naomi Joy. Adam would take Naomi Joy to Denise's home every Wednesday morning on his way to work, then pick her up again on his way back in the evening. Denise had fallen in love with this Asian beauty from the first time she saw her, four months ago. Denise's ten-year-old daughter, Tamera, felt the same way, and was excited to spend time with the baby before and after school. This would be a time Maggie could enjoy a full day of quiet and play with Jason; as well as providing a caring environment for Naomi Joy. Denise loved holding Naomi Joy and did so all day long!

Maggie started meeting with another member of the church, Ellen, who was a psychiatric nurse at the local hospital. Ellen helped her work through some of her own feelings, and to get some medical intervention, an antidepressant that might help her cope better.

These things did ease the pressure, although Maggie found Thursdays quite trying. Naomi Joy loved being held all day on Wednesday, and spent Thursday in worse shape than she had been before. Maggie simply could not hold the baby all day, and Naomi Joy insisted that she be held! The battle continued, although Maggie felt some relief by the measures this team had put together. There just might be a silver lining to these dark clouds that had gather around Maggie!

◆   ◆   ◆

Adam enjoyed talking with Denise about Naomi Joy. Tamera obviously loved this little princess as well. It was difficult to understand why Maggie was having such a hard time with her—everyone else absolutely loved her. She was so cute, even charming. Talking with Denise was such an encouragement. Adam talked to Maggie about having Denise, her husband and daughter over for a dinner meal—it would be great to interact more with this family. Adam hoped that Denise could be an encouragement for Maggie—Denise certainly had a way with the baby!

Maggie agreed that it was a good idea. Maybe they could talk and work out some things so it would be easier on Naomi Joy coming back on Wednesday evenings. Maggie had always enjoyed Denise and a meal together would be a great thing.

Maggie decided that it would be the best to prepare a simple meal ~ just about anything was an overwhelming task right now. She peeled the potatoes and watched Jason work on his own potato. He loved to help in the kitchen. He chattered excitedly as he "worked". He liked Tamera, too, and was talking about all the things he would show her when she arrived. Maggie turned to look at Naomi Joy sitting in her little high chair nearby. She was quiet and content right now because of the cheese on her tray, in her hands, and stuffed in her mouth.

Naomi Joy loved to eat ~ it was one of her happiest times. The baby had to have something in front of her, something in her left hand, while she stuffed the food in with her right. Many times, Naomi Joy would cry because she couldn't get any more in her mouth. She had too much in there to swallow, and refused to spit any out. If Maggie removed any, Naomi Joy would become hysterical.

"Food is love". Maggie had heard that once somewhere. For Naomi Joy, this certainly seemed to be true. Mommy was not love, that was for sure! Daddy was a great guy, but it seemed like Naomi Joy used Daddy to get to Mommy. Naomi Joy had Daddy wrapped around her little finger, and he just could not see why Maggie struggled so with her. This put a wedge between Adam and Maggie that was driving them further and further apart. Naomi Joy did seem somewhat attached to Jason, but didn't truly connect with anyone else. But food; yes, for Naomi Joy, food was love.

Maggie sighed. A tear slowly trickled down her cheek. She angrily brushed it away. How many tears had she wept for this child? When would it all end? Even when Naomi Joy was quietly eating, it seemed like Maggie could hear the screaming. She had started calling Naomi Joy "the scream machine" because she heard little else from her. Maggie refused to shed another tear that night. She continued to peel potatoes and "listen" to Jason rattle on.

◆   ◆   ◆

The next morning, Pastor Daniel called again. His question was so odd. "Maggie, is Naomi Joy alright?"

"She is her usual self…" Why would he ask that? Very strange.

"And you, Maggie, are you alright?"

"Sure, I'm fine. We had Denise and her family over last night for dinner. We had a great time ~ really enjoyed them. I feel good, having friends over and visiting."

"Hmmm. Denise told me that Tamera was helping you change Naomi Joy. Naomi Joy was wiggling, and you slapped her on the tummy. When Denise looked later, she had a handprint on her there. Is this true? She was concerned and wanted me to follow up on it."

Maggie spent a few moments thinking. A handprint? She couldn't *remember* hitting Naomi Joy. Surely she would remember such a thing! But why would Tamera lie? She was just a little girl ~ and a wonderful little girl at that! Surely she wouldn't lie. Maggie was confused. How could she answer this strange question?

"Well, Daniel, I can't imagine Tamera lying. She is an honest little thing, but, I don't remember hitting Naomi Joy."

"Would you go check for me ~ check Naomi Joy and see if there's anything there?"

Obediently, Maggie looked at little Naomi Joy. She lifted the baby's dress to look at her tummy. "No, Daniel, there is nothing there. She has the rash, of course, that she always has. But that's all I see..."

She could hear the pastor's sigh of relief. "Good. That's all I needed to know. So ~ how are you *really*?"

Maggie was in shock. She spoke briefly with Daniel ~ she was too shook up to talk. After hanging up, she sat down heavily on the kitchen chair. Her eyes wandered to Naomi Joy. Another tear slid down her cheek. No, it couldn't be true...could it? She couldn't remember hitting Naomi Joy. She could remember Tamera helping her change the baby. She tried to think back over the sequence of events. Tamera had helped her with the powder, wipes...Naomi Joy was pretty good about changing ~ she didn't wiggle hardly at all. She hated being dirty and wanted that diaper off. She rarely fought changing. Yet, Tamera wasn't inclined to lie. Maybe she did hit the baby? Did she? NO! She couldn't have. Could she?

"My God!" cried out Maggie's voice, "My God! Am I finally insane? She's driven me crazy! I don't know if I did it or not! I'm nuts—I've lost my mind! I didn't hit her! I know I didn't hit her! Did I? Did I, God? Did I hit my baby? NO! NO! NO! I am NOT crazy! I didn't hit her, I didn't hurt her, I didn't..." Sobs stopped her from screaming out any more. She was scared...so scared. She MUST be going crazy! The sobs continued to shake her body. She looked up and saw Naomi Joy looking at her. She wasn't screaming. She wasn't moving. She just sat there and stared. Maggie watched her through her tears and the doubts as to her own sanity. The thought was fleeting and she tried to dismiss it. *I must be crazy. I can't even remember any more. I must be crazy. How could a mother ha....* Quickly, she erased even the trace of the last thought, laid her head upon her folded arms on the kitchen table and wept.

February, 1982

Maggie's birthday was coming up! Adam and Jason tried to make it special the last couple of years. It had been such a fun time for the three of them. Maggie wondered what they were cooking up this time. Surely she could use a smile about now! Things were slightly better. She still had that one day off a week, but it was followed by another day of pure hell. And Naomi Joy finally realized that her momma had responsibilities other than rocking a baby. Maggie noticed a weight gain that appeared to be a side effect of the antidepressant. Although she found *that* depressing, she was able to handle her circumstances more effectively. Equally as important, she had completely stopped drinking. The baby was still the screaming, but it seemed to be mostly at night. Now that Naomi Joy was crawling and getting around better on her own, she was a more content.

Poor Adam was starting to show the marks of stress. He was almost afraid to leave for work, not knowing what he would come home to. Fortunately, the job at the hospital an hour away gave him a good excuse to be away. He even put in some overtime rather than be amidst the tension at home. Sometimes he wondered if he wanted to go home at all. Maggie seemed slightly better to him as well, but far from the cheerful, well-organized woman he had met and married almost seven years ago. Things were drastically different since Naomi Joy had come. His wife rarely smiled and was exhausted all of the time. She certainly had no energy for him at the end of the day. And on weekends, she expected him to practically run the home single handedly. It was definitely not his idea of relaxing! He used to look forward to coming home, to spending the weekend with his family. Not so now; not so now…

He reminded himself, her birthday was drawing near, and he really ought to make an effort to make it special. It would be nice to have a special dinner and a thoughtful gift. Earplugs crossed his mind. However, she would probably appreciate flowers more! Jason could help cook dinner, a chore he absolutely loved. Or, Adam thought, maybe he should take the family out to dinner. That was a privilege they seldom enjoyed; maybe it would be just what Maggie needed. Yes, a dinner out would be perfect!

23

It did turn out to be a good idea. Naomi Joy loved being out and admired by everyone around her. She was dressed in one of the beautiful dresses Maggie made; she had a cute little ponytail with a ribbon in her hair. What a doll, thought Adam—and most of the people in the restaurant! The waitresses were fighting good-naturedly over who could wait on them, or bring them water, or offer dessert. Naomi Joy put on a great show for them, smiling and laughing! She had such an adorable laugh! As long as there was food on her tray, she was content.

Jason was so animated. Adam had to laugh as he remembered that little monkey standing up in his chair, pointing a finger at a heavy-set lady across the room. His shocked voice squeaked, "Look, Mommy, that lady is *smoking!* She is going to die!" Maggie had quickly seated him, hushing him. They were all embarrassed, but looking back on the incident, it really *was* funny!

It was good to laugh. There was so little laughter around the house any more, although it helped having Naomi Joy going to Denise's house once a week. Maggie seemed better when he returned with Naomi Joy on Wednesday evening, full of stories of her time with Jason. But Thursday she was down again, and things worsened again until the following Wednesday evening. A man ought to enjoy coming home—every day, not just once a week.

Adam sighed; maybe a change in scenery would help. He had been called by a "head hunter" about a job in Denver. Would it help to move the family back home, back to Colorado? Maggie had often mentioned going back a few years ago. It hadn't come up in a long time. Maybe he should talk about it some more, see what it was all about. It was for an airline. It looked attractive. He wouldn't say anything to Maggie about it yet. If she got her hopes up, and then he had to disappoint her...Well, she was so depressed already. Sometimes he wondered if she would still be there when he got home. He was sure the drinking had stopped. She was on medication, but she was still so depressed.

What else could he do for her? What in the world did she want from him? He was doing all he could ~ taking Naomi Joy to Denise's house every week, helping out on weekends with the baby (almost a year old already!), working hard, keeping a roof over their heads, food in their mouths. If it weren't for his little princess, he wondered if he would bother to go home at night. Why, why did Maggie struggle so much with Naomi Joy?

◆   ◆   ◆

Maggie knew, in spite of the day off and Adam's help, that she just couldn't go on any longer. She was going absolutely crazy. She was staying sober, and some how making it through each day, but getting up each morning was becoming more and more difficult. No sleep most of the night, struggling through each day, falling into bed exhausted, only to not sleep again was a routine that she could no longer endure. The crying just wouldn't stop unless someone else was there for Naomi Joy to "win over". All night, most of the day…Crying and crying…Everyone loved Naomi Joy, finding her delightful. There must be something terribly wrong with me, Maggie thought over and over. There has to be a change.

Maggie talked frequently with Pastor Daniel. She called him again and confessed her feelings of inadequacy, and her fear that she couldn't make it even one more day. Together, they came up with a plan, presenting it to Adam that evening. Naomi Joy would go and stay with the family of a church elder for two weeks. During that time, Maggie could rest. Hopefully after a couple of weeks, she would be able to handle things once again.

As Maggie packed Naomi Joy's things, she caressed each item, wondering what in the world was wrong. Naomi Joy was a beautiful baby, and was moving around on her own now. She was happy and playful with Adam now and there were moments of fun even for Maggie. But those times were rare, and it seemed that the hurting times were just overwhelming. Little Naomi Joy's first birthday was coming, and Maggie had really thought that they would find a way to live together by now…

"Jason!" Maggie called.

"Yes, Mama?" Jason came in from the other room to see what was happening.

Maggie turned to her son. She looked at him carefully. Why couldn't Naomi Joy have just a little bit of his joy? Why could she find such satisfaction in this son, and be so utterly useless when it came to Naomi Joy? Jason loved to laugh, play games, be read to, and play in the sandbox ~ everything was so much fun for him. Naomi Joy seemed to bond with him ~ no one else. Maybe Naomi Joy saw in Jason some of what Maggie appreciated in him.

Maggie knelt down so she was eye level with Jason. "Sweetheart, I need some rest ~ a little vacation. I can't sleep like you can! You sleep right through Naomi Joy's crying, don't you?"

Jason laughed. "I could sleep through a tornado. You told me so!"

Maggie laughed too. "Yep ~ that's my Jason! You could even sleep through a tornado! But I can't; so when Naomi Joy cries, I wake up and can't go to sleep. That's part of why I have been so tired and grumpy lately."

Before she could continue, Jason threw his arms around Maggie's neck with a big hug. She loved getting his hugs ~ since he turned a year old, he just wasn't cuddly any more. He told her he was a "big boy" now, and far to busy for cuddling ~ except on those rare occasions he was sick! "You aren't grumpy Mama! Let's go play with my Legos. You can help me build a big airplane!"

"Good idea, Jason. We have fun building with your Legos. But first, I have to finish here. Do you know what I'm doing?"

"You are packing clothes for Naomi Joy."

"That's right, Big Guy! Naomi Joy is going to stay with our friends, the Grainers, for a couple of weeks. That way I can sleep at night, and we can do more things together. Won't that be fun?! Then Naomi Joy will come home after our little vacation together. Of course, we wouldn't want her to be gone *too* long would we? You'd miss her, wouldn't you?"

"Sure, I'll miss her. But she'll come home soon, right, Mama? And we'll have a vacation together? Just you and me?"

Maggie grinned. "And Daddy when he comes home from work, of course! What will we do while Naomi Joy is at Grainer's?"

Jason had lots of ideas. He chattered while Maggie finished packing. Naomi Joy watched Jason as he talked. Maggie smiled to herself. It would be a good break!

That evening, when Adam got home from work, they all piled in the car and drove over to Grainer's home. Mrs. Grainer grinned as she took Naomi Joy from her father. It was difficult for Adam to let Naomi Joy go ~ he spent some time playing peek-a-boo with her and watched her laugh. She had such a cute laugh ~ everyone loved it. Mrs. Grainer's children gathered around to watch the show and see if they could get her to laugh as well. Maggie and Adam quickly and quietly escorted Jason out while Naomi Joy was entertained by, and entertained, the three children and their parents. Great people, the Grainers. Naomi Joy was in good hands.

"Let's stop for a little supper, okay, Jason?!" Adam said.

"Oh, yes! That's a great way to start a vacation, right Mama?!"

Maggie laughed. "Indeed it is, Son. Doesn't Daddy have great ideas?"

"Well, then, I guess it's unanimous!" responded Adam.

That night, Maggie slept soundly for the first time in almost six months. She could have slept for three days, she thought as she stretched in her warm waterbed. Adam had already gotten up, showered and dressed. "Good morning, Sleepyhead! How did you sleep?"

Maggie stretched even more. "With my eyes closed ~ *all night long!*" Adam laughed at her joke ~ even if she did steal it from him!

"Well, how about you stay right there, and I'll go get Jason. I've heard our little early riser already. He can cuddle with you."

Adam left and came back carrying Jason. He looked adorable in his little sleeper and his hair tousled. What a doll! Adam set him down on the bed. "Let's tickle Mommy, okay Jason?! Get her!!!" The three of them laughed and tickled and played for a few minutes before Adam had to leave for work. Jason laughed and laughed with his little boy laugh. Maggie loved it. Now <u>this</u> is what life ought to be!

After a bit, Maggie asked if Jason was ready for a little breakfast. He was trying to walk around on the waterbed without falling down. He plopped down on his bottom, increasing the motion of the bed, much to his delight. "Pancakes! Pancakes! We **love** pancakes!"

Maggie decided that, for just today, they could cook and eat in their pajamas. Why not? They were on vacation!

Gradually, as the first few days passed, Maggie began to feel like her old self again. She was able to sing when she got up in the morning, go to the park and play Frisbee with the dog, Snooker. Jason enjoyed running in the snow, building a snowman; and even a "snow fort" from which he could attack his mother with snowballs. It was as if she had never been depressed at all. They had picnics on the living room floor, made play dough, painted pictures and "wrote" letters to Grandma. Adam would come home each evening and enjoy playing with Jason and spend time with the wife he had thought was gone forever. Perhaps all she needed was a break ~ she seemed to be back to "normal", but he sure did miss his little princess. Adam took it upon himself to call every other night to find out how Naomi Joy was doing.

The two weeks were almost over before Maggie could bring herself to call and check on Naomi Joy. She could hardly believe the time was almost over. She dialed the phone slowly; not sure she wanted to talk with Mrs. Grainer.

"Hello, Grainer's."

"Good morning, Laura. This is Maggie. I am calling to see how our little one is doing!" She tried to put some enthusiasm into her voice.

"Maggie! It's good to hear from you. It was good to see you in church the other day, but I just didn't get a chance to talk with you. Little Naomi Joy is doing wonderfully. The children, Don and I have really enjoyed her. She has been playing with Kirk. The girls and Kirk have really doted on her."

Maggie couldn't decide if she was glad or not. Why was Naomi Joy so great for everyone else, but…"It's probably been good for Naomi Joy. She does love the attention, doesn't she?"

"Well, that part has been…Just a second, Maggie! Whoa, Naomi Joy just stood up in the middle of the living room! Look at that! She is balanced perfectly! I can't believe it. Wait! Maggie, she is walking! She is actually walking! Oh, my!"

Maggie couldn't believe it. Naomi Joy wouldn't even pull up on furniture! Now she just stands up and walks! "What is she doing, what is she doing, Laura?"

It sounded like Laura was about to cry. "Maggie, she walked over to the couch, turned around and…And she smiled, Maggie!"

Now, Maggie *really* was surprised. Naomi Joy smiled spontaneously ~ no one tickling her or making faces ~ she smiled because she was pleased with herself. Maggie let her breathe out. "She smiled?"

Now Laura *was* crying. "Yes, Maggie, she smiled!"

Maggie and Laura talked for a bit longer. After hanging up, Maggie sat down heavily. She had missed her daughter's first steps! This was a major mile marker, but another had been there to clap and cheer the baby on! Yet, she had to acknowledge that this must be a little miracle. Naomi Joy had never before smiled because of something she had done herself. Maybe she just wanted to walk ~ by herself. Maybe she just wanted some independence. Was that what had been the problem all this time? And to simply stand up and walk ~ whoever heard of such a thing? Yes, it must be a little miracle! Maggie smiled. A little miracle!

Spring ~ 1982

Naomi Joy returned a few days later. The first couple of days went well. It was amazing to watch her walk! Jason delighted in the new development. He would stand in front of her and challenge her to come to him for a hug, a tickle or a toy. When she toddled over, he laughed so hard she would laugh as well. They played inside and outside, letting Naomi Joy experience walking on the wooden floor, tiled floor, carpeting, sidewalk and uneven ground. It brought much enjoyment to both of them.

Adam loved coming home from work and watching Naomi Joy as she demonstrated her newly discovered ability. He would encourage, chortle, clap and laugh while she toddled around. Maggie watched and laughed as well. It was indeed a little miracle.

It didn't take too long, however, before the newness wore off and Naomi Joy began to display the same old behaviors. She consistently pushed away from Maggie when she tried to hug her daughter; yet when Adam held her, Naomi Joy would cuddle into him and stare at her mother. Maggie felt that stare. What in the world was it all about? Maggie would puzzle over it ~ could it be…well, disdain? That's how it looked. Yet, how could such a thing be? The child was barely a year old. Maggie would shake her head. She must be imagining it. It was just foolishness, nothing else. It would not be for many years that she would learn about <u>RAD</u>, <u>R</u>eactive <u>A</u>ttachment <u>D</u>isorder[1].

Adam continued to follow up on the job possibility in Colorado. He was sure a change of scenery would help Maggie regain a sense of balance, a sense of her old joy. She had always been so joyful, when he met her, as she graduated from college, moved to Utah for the job at the deaf school, as she worked for three years with those "sweet babies" of hers, waited for Jason to be born. There had been some hard times just before they moved to Utah ~ but that move worked wonders. She had so much loved her job, and Jason's arrival had added to her joy. At the school, she was called "Pollyanna", and comments about her "rose colored glasses" still circulated there, as well as in their church. Over the past few months she changed, and others were beginning to notice. She was no Pollyanna now!

Since the first move had helped so much, surely returning to Colorado and family would help.

They had grown so much in Utah. Their faith was constantly challenged. As followers of the Jesus portrayed in the Bible, they now were forced to study their beliefs, holding them up for close examination. What did the Bible say about His birth? Did God have a physical form that actually conceived the Child? Could it be that He did **not** die for **all** sin; that there are some sins for which His blood could **not** atone? Was it true that man becomes a god himself, continuing to pro-create in order to populate a new world? These, and many other questions had to have answers.

Adam and Maggie found those answers as they read and studied their Bible. They determined to stand on and hold firm to their faith, their conviction of the Truth they discovered there. Now, however, they held those beliefs out of their <u>personal</u> confidence. Jesus did come, fully God yet fully man, to die for all sin! Adam was relieved to find that he wouldn't become a god himself. Maggie was even more so! Imagine spending eternity having babies! They had decided to attend a small fellowship. That very smallness of the church had contributed to their growth as well. They had to accept an active part in the church, since they had all of forty people (including children!) when they had first arrived. They had "gone through" several pastors since they had arrived, eight years prior! The first simply moved on. Two pastors came after that. Adam thought back to their time with Brad and Rich.

That had been when the church really started to grow! Rich and Brad were incredibly dynamic! They caused their "flock" to begin seriously studying the Word. They taught classes in Greek and Hebrew, Biblical history and archeol-

---

1.   Reactive Attachment Disorder, or RAD, is a condition in which an individual has difficulty forming healthy bonds with his/her caregivers. As a result, he/she is unable to show affection for or trust others. Because they do not trust, they fail to develop a conscience. The following list identifies some, not all of the symptoms the children may display: Superficially charming and engaging; Affectionate with strangers; Sometimes tries to leave with strangers; (Continued on next page.)

Fire setting; No conscience; No cause and effect thinking; Refuses, resists, or is uncomfortable with affection on caretakers' terms; Harming and/or killing small animals; Destruction of property (their own and/or others; Self mutilation; Hoarding, gorging, eating disorders or hiding food; Intense control battles; Fascination with weapons, blood or gore; Crazy lying; and Caretakers who feel like giving up or feel hostile toward the child.

ogy...They challenged the people in the congregation ~ and the culture around them!

It was Brad who flew them out in his little four-seater airplane to get Jason from Arkansas when he was born! How funny that whole trip had been! Adam smiled as he remembered their adventures.

Brad preached his sermon that Sunday. Then they took off in his little Cessna for Arkansas. He and Maggie were so excited ~ the trip was well laid out and they would see their new son on Monday! First, they would fly from Ogden to a small airport outside of Sedalia, Colorado. All three of them would spend the night with Maggie's mother. Then, in the morning, after Maggie's mom returned them to the airport, they would head out for Arkansas!

The first leg of the trip went just fine ~ a unique way to start out the new year. Who would have guessed that the cold would affect the battery in the airplane? No problem! Adam would work on turning the propeller, Brad would work the ignition, and Maggie's mother would sit in her car, while they jumped the battery from her car. What a sight they must have made. That "backwash" from the prop was the beginning of the horrible cold with which he had returned from the trip. But, at least they got it running and took off for Arkansas.

Much of the trip there was uneventful, until Brad decided to stop for gas. The sudden drop put Adam and Maggie's stomachs in their throats! Then, after getting gas, Brad decided that he didn't need to go up too high since they must be close to their destination. However, he wasn't certain *just* where it was. So, he played "Sky King", buzzing the water towers to read the town names of each city over which they passed. This did *not* help the stomach problems much! In fact, when they finally landed, Adam and Maggie wanted to kiss the nice, firm earth! There they were met by the gentleman from the school that was providing the care for the mother of the baby. He would take them to the hospital to pick up the baby, then to the motel to spend the night before taking off for Colorado the next day.

Brad, Adam and Maggie had to wait in the van while their "host" went in for the baby and his nurse. It seemed like they had to wait forever before the nurse appeared, holding the precious bundle. Maggie reached out for the baby, anxious for the nurse to place him in her waiting arms. Adam remembered leaning over and looking into the face of their newborn son as Maggie unwrapped him. He was beautiful, of course.

Adam and Maggie remembered proper priorities when they arrived at the motel. The first thing they did was lay that baby boy on the bed, unwrap him, take off his little outfit and marvel at the miracle of this child. Five toes on each bare foot. Five fingers on each little hand. What tiny ears, an adorable nose, and that perfectly formed mouth! Even the little tuft of red hair at the nape of his neck was perfect!

Of course, Brad had a different set of priorities. Dinner should come first! They were told that there was a restaurant at the hotel. When Brad called, they found out it was closed. No problem. They had also been informed that the small town had a Taxi service ~ they could call a taxi, get a ride to a pizza place, ride back and have dinner. Not so. The taxi company was no longer in service ~ since the preceding week! Brad was not daunted. He walked the distance to the pizza place, ordered dinner, started up a conversation with a lady there, and by the time the it was ready, she was ready to give the pizza and Brad a ride back to the hotel. She didn't even require a personal view of the new baby!!!

When Brad finally returned, the baby was once again clothed and Adam and Maggie had realized just how hungry they were. They quietly ate as the baby slept. Then Brad laughed. "Wait a minute! We are already training this baby to require quiet in order to sleep! Stop whispering! Let's just talk!"

The advice must have been right. Once at home, Maggie would become tired of waiting for Jason to wake up so she could play with him. She didn't want to wake him up ~ that certainly wasn't good parenting! So, she would vacuum the dining room, right off the nursery. When that didn't work, she'd open his door. That was ineffective, so she would vacuum the nursery, including directly under his crib. Jason *didn't* need quiet in order to sleep from the very beginning!

The return trip was filled with even more adventure. When they tried to take off to fly home, the plane was heavier than when they had set out ~ now that they had Jason, plus the Christmas gifts from both sets of grandparents. Well, it seems the plane was just a bit too heavy to fight the headwind. Every time Brad tried to move, the nose of the airplane went up in the air and they couldn't move. Brad took charge and had Adam walk to the other end of the runway. That made quite a bit of difference. Maggie moved into the front of the plane to balance the weight. Then Brad taxied down to that end to meet Adam. In this way, they could take off with rather than against the wind. Arriving at the other end of the runway, Brad turned the plane around and had Adam get back in out of the whistling cold air that had left him incredibly chilled. That, and the jump start of the plane before, standing in the "backwash" from the propeller, was the start of one of the worst colds Adam had *ever* had! They did finally make it as far as Colorado again, to make another "lay over" at the home of Maggie's mom.

Maggie's mother was so thrilled with her first grandchild. She had to share the infant when Adam's parents came over to see him. Jason was also <u>their</u> first grandchild. This would be one spoiled little boy! However, when Adam's parents went home and Jason was ready for his night feeding, grandma took over. When Maggie returned with the warmed bottle, the baby was gone! She found him, looking up into his grandmother's face, secure in her bed. She firmly stated that <u>she</u> would be feeding the baby. Maggie settled herself on the bed and watched happily as her mother fed her new baby boy.

The remainder of the trip back home was relatively uneventful. The new baby slept whenever the plane was in motion, and woke up when it stopped! He was such a good baby, and the two pastors adopted him as their own as well. In fact, baby Jason belonged to the whole church.

Adam didn't have long to wait. The job with the airline in Denver came through! He could talk with Maggie about it now. She would be so excited. They would finally be back with family. He was so relieved. Things had gotten so tense around the house.

Maggie was elated about the news. She looked forward to the move. She loved change, new places, new people, a new home; but it meant putting their house on the market and that would be a new experience. They had the house ready quickly; it was a small home, a "starter home".

Adam was hoping the house would sell, but the airline job demanded that he move to Denver right away. Maggie's mom said he could stay with her until he found a house. Maggie stayed behind with the children until the house in Utah sold. In the meantime, he could fly out every weekend to spend time with the family at no cost.

In a lot of ways, this was a very happy time for them. Adam would fly out and arrive late Friday night. Maggie left the children with a sitter and met him in Salt Lake City for a midnight breakfast. She loved going out for breakfast in the middle of the night. After spending the night alone, they picked up the children and had the weekend together. Then Adam would fly back to Denver late Sunday night, looking forward to the next weekend. Maggie felt like they were dating again. It was wonderful! That lasted three months. Then the house sold; they could stay with Maggie's mom until Adam found a home. The family was together again.

The agency refused to allow the Naomi Joy's adoption to be finalized. The six-month waiting period was up, but the "trauma" of the move, new job, and a new home made finalization unwise. They assigned a new caseworker in Denver to handle the case there. Little did Adam or Maggie know that the trouble was going to escalate far beyond anything they could even imagine.

When they all moved in with Maggie's mom she was delighted to have the company. Maggie had so many memories there; she wanted to share them with the children. Too bad the horse had long since been gone! Maggie had loved riding and knew that Jason would enjoy it as well. Jason had been on the horse only once, and he had been so little. Naomi Joy had never seen the horse, but Maggie thought that the little girl would be delighted with such a huge animal. Maggie smiled as she remembered the first time that Adam had ever come to meet her parents. She was out riding, high on the hill when she saw him driving up. She raced on the old mare, arriving at the barn about the same time his car had pulled into the driveway.

One warm afternoon, Maggie decided to take the children to the beaver pond where she and her own four siblings had spent so much time. The beavers had moved their pond and the surrounding scenery was a little bit different, but the water was warm, and not *too* deep. Maggie gave the children turns. First, Naomi Joy entered the pond with Mom while Jason waded and played at the edge. Then, Naomi Joy played at the edge while Jason paddled around in the deeper part with Mom. The children laughed and squealed, and Maggie laughed with them.

It was Jason's turn again, and Maggie was helping him float. Jason hated water in his ears, and putting his head into it was not his idea of a great time. Maggie decided to just let him play, knowing that as he relaxed, floating would come naturally to her budding athlete. She turned slightly to make sure Naomi Joy was safe. Naomi Joy was not to be seen!

Maggie viewed the whole scene quickly, while she took Jason back to shore. Where had the little one gone? Maggie had never considered the beaver dam as a dangerous place, but suddenly it was a place that held great danger. How quickly Naomi Joy could have toddled off into the willow trees, or fallen into the water! Where was she? As she walked and looked, there was Naomi Joy, just under the surface, her eyes as big as saucers. Maggie reached down and pulled Naomi Joy to the surface, where she smiled happily. She had been "swimming" without help! Maggie shook her head,. "Little One, nothing stops you, does it? Not being able to swim won't stop you for one second from trying!"

Maggie held Naomi Joy close in spite of her struggle to go "swim" again. Her sigh of relief was deep. "Let's try again, but let's stay closer together, okay?!" Naomi Joy couldn't be happier. The water was fine, the sunshine was warm and, by gum, *she* could swim!

When Grandma and Daddy got home that evening, Jason was bubbling with information ~ and Naomi Joy toddled after her big brother with much enthusiasm.

"You should have seen Naomi Joy, Daddy! Grandma, she can swim **all by herself!** I saw her!"

Naomi Joy was jumping up and down and clapping her tiny little hands together. "Yes, yes, yes!"

Maggie explained, with a great deal of help and animation by Naomi Joy and Jason. They all laughed together as she described seeing Naomi Joy's eyes, just as big as they could be, looking at her through the water. Naomi Joy opened her eyes as wide as she could to demonstrate, and clapped her hands as everyone laughed.

Although the country air and daily walks seemed so good for the family, Adam and Maggie were delighted when they found a little house for their family. And little it was ~ nine hundred square feet to be exact. It was truly a cracker box, much smaller than their home in Ogden, but they could afford it and it had three bedrooms somehow crammed into that little space.

The back yard was big and very green, the lawn being shaded by a huge tree. Three blocks away was a nice big park with a great play area for the children. The commute to work for Adam was not as long as it had been with his former job in Utah. Now, he'd have more time at home with his family. The house would do, for now!

Maggie was pleased. A home of her own again in Denver meant that now they could start looking for a church, making their own new friends, get settled down, and maybe begin some sort of normal routine. It would be good indeed!

PART II

Warfare?

Strange things just kept happening. Maggie tried to think back to the first whisper of this strange stuff happening. She could remember once, back in Utah, when the collie mix dog, Snooker, had laid down in front of the bedroom door, and growled. Maggie had tried to coax Snooker away from the doorway, but he refused to move. He must have laid there for forty-five minutes, growling menacingly at the bedroom, not moving a muscle. After awhile, he had finally pulled away, but refused to enter the bedroom for several days ~ even though he normally slept in the room. Strange.

It was the next day that Maggie had been working in the children's' room, cleaning, and suddenly the blender turned itself on. She had thought it odd at the time. When Adam had gotten home, she had told him about it. Adam had checked out the blender, and couldn't find anything wrong with it ~ and it never happened again.

The next day, the picture in the dining room jumped off the wall. Well, it didn't actually _jump_ off; it just fell off. But the funny thing was that no one was anywhere around it at the time ~ the children were playing in the bedroom and Maggie had been sitting and watching them. It startled them all ~ Maggie put it back up, and it never happened again!

She tried to think if anything else had happened there in Utah. She couldn't remember anything specific…

The day at Mom's house was truly bizarre. Maggie had been standing in the kitchen, putting away the silverware at her mother's house. No one else was there ~ the others had all gone for a walk, Adam, Naomi Joy, Jason and Grandma. Maggie was thinking about the upcoming move, when someone (thing?) slapped her so hard on the back that she fell forward and had to catch herself on the counter. She spun around, and saw ~ no one. There wasn't a sound in the house. Snooker had gone on the walk with the others, so he wasn't even there to make the floor creak ~ let alone…Spooky…

Maggie decided that it would be a good thing when they got into the new house. Hopefully these unusual things would stop. She certainly hoped so. She couldn't decide if she was actually going crazy or if these weird things were real.

No other witnesses (with the exception of the children and the dog—and who would believe a dog???), had been present at *any* of these events ~ the bedroom, blender, picture and now this slap…Come to think of it, why would anyone believe *her* at this point?

◆   ◆   ◆

The new house was indeed small, but it was cozy. When all their furniture was in, arranged and used once again, it became home. Having a park close by wasn't quite as wonderful as a beaver dam and acreage, but it was certainly good enough. Maggie "needed" the outdoors. She hated feeling closed in, staying in any house too much. She relished having the warm sunshine on her face. She did need that; without it she found it easy to be depressed. They walked to the park to play nearly every day, and the sunshine break helped her maintain.

Naomi Joy had a "thing" about cleanliness. She absolutely hated to get dirty. She stayed away from anything that might possibly get her pretty clothes or dainty hands soiled. This particular day was of unequaled beauty. Colorado has the most beautiful blue skies, thought Maggie as they walked. Even in the dead of winter there was always at least a promise of coming sunshine. It was warm today; there wasn't even a breeze. Just exactly the kind of day one needs to go for a walk with two cute children!

Jason made straight for the slide, of course. Being such a big guy now, he easily climbed the ladder and shrieked all the way down. He was a bit cautious, ever since that time in Utah when he had missed a step and fell, straddling the ladder. Crying, he had limped over to her. "It hurts, Mommy! It hurts so bad! Please make it all better!" She felt rather helpless. There are some "owies" that only time heals. He absolutely loved coaxing his collie, Snooker, up to the top of the slide and encouraging him to go down! Everyone laughed at that trick!

Snooker was great at catching a Frisbee as well. One time, they threw the Frisbee and yelled, "Heads up!" to a nine-year-old boy as it sailed over his head. As the boy looked up, Snooker sailed over his head as well, catching the Frisbee in the air, dropping to the ground, and carelessly trotting back with it. The boy fell over in shock seeing that big dog jump over his head! Maggie never got tired of watching that silly dog! On ice, he was an absolute hoot! He braced his front legs as he approached his objective, and picked it up as he slid past, swung around and headed back for the next throw. They NEVER went to the park without Snooker. Maggie was glad she had the children now. The children at the park called her "Jason's mommy" instead of "Snooker's mommy". Somehow, "Jason's mommy" had a much better sound to it!

They all watched Snooker and Jason go down the slide several times, being careful to avoid the mud at the bottom of the slide. Naomi Joy decided that it was her turn. Maggie helped her to the ladder. Jason followed her up, declaring knowledgeably, "It is a big brother's responsibility, Mom!". Maggie waited at the bottom. Naomi Joy balanced at the top, sat down, and started down. She squealed in delight. Maggie caught her, and they repeated the whole process.

It wasn't until the fourth time that Naomi Joy decided she was ready to try going down without a "catcher" waiting at the bottom. Maggie watched with some uneasiness. She stood close by, just in case.

Naomi Joy wasn't prepared for the mud at the bottom, even after watching big brother avoid it. Splash! She landed on her feet and hands somehow! Maggie giggled a little, Jason's eyes grew several sizes, but Naomi Joy stood there in shock, looking at her hands. Mud coated them. Horrors! Her hands were *dirty!!!*

Maggie and Jason stood motionless for a moment, waiting for Naomi Joy's reaction. She looked up from her hands, her face crumbling as tears began to fall. "Dirty! Mommy, my hands are dirty!"

"It's okay, Honey. Let's just wipe them on your pants. Then your hands will be okay!" Maggie helped Naomi Joy wipe her hands on her little pants. Naomi Joy then looked from her hands to her pants.

"NO, Mommy! Hands are dirty! *Pants* are dirty!"

Oh, my, thought Maggie. What now??? She thought quickly. The swings! Naomi Joy loves the swings. That'll take her mind off the mud. Maggie led her daughter to the swings. "Let's swing, Baby. That'll be fun!" She lifted Naomi Joy into the swing, made sure she was holding on, and gave her a gentle push. Surely this would take the toddler's mind off the mud!

Naomi Joy looked up briefly. She looked down at her legs, now closer to her face because of sitting in the swing! A very loud cry issued forth, *"Dirty! Naomi Joy dirty!!!"*

There was nothing to be done. Maggie, Snooker, Jason and Naomi Joy's day at the park ended early. It was definitely bath time!

◆   ◆   ◆

The new caseworker, Sally, somehow didn't seem to believe Maggie or Adam. They repeated over and over again that they wanted to adopt this little girl. Sally repeated again, "There just seems to be this…uncertainty about you. I am simply offering you the opportunity to have an 'out'. If you are at all unsure, I am giving you the chance to change your mind about keeping Naomi Joy."

Adam was shocked. "We have had this child for well over a year. She is our daughter. Why would you even suggest we surrender her?"

Sally looked from father to mother. The father did seem committed to this child. It was the mother...Sally sensed something there, a lack of caring? No, that wasn't really it. She did sincerely care. Perhaps a lack of love? No, there did seem to be a "love bond". But, there just was...something...

"I am simply asking..." Sally trailed off, and then moved on to a new subject.

◆   ◆   ◆

There was one thing that Maggie particularly liked about the new little house. When the furnace kicked in, it made this wonderful roar that masked the baby's crying at night. Maggie would snuggle down under the covers, pull in closer to Adam, bury her face in the pillow, and actually sleep when their furnace began its rumbling lullaby. It was never long enough. When it turned off, she could hear the torturous crying again. Crying, crying, crying, but for a few minutes, wonderful, glorious minutes, the crying could not be heard and Maggie could catch twenty...thirty minutes of sleep. Ahhhh, the furnace was on. Sleep. Sleep.

◆   ◆   ◆

Maggie started working with an organization in Denver that helped and encouraged people who had been or were involved in any type of abuse. It was fascinating, and she was slowly developing some friendships. They were different from the relationships she was forming within the new church family. It gave Maggie a challenge that she was enjoying. Occasionally Adam accompanied her and he found it interesting ~ but not his "thing". He encouraged Maggie, though. It was good for her to have an outside interest; or was distraction a better word?

The director of the organization, Sharon, seemed to be a good sounding board. She listened to Maggie and gave her suggestions as to how to handle Naomi Joy. It helped Maggie have a sense of balance.

After awhile, Sharon gave Maggie an "assignment". There was a woman who had grown up with abuse, raised her own children in a harsh manner, and was now a nanny for a local family. The woman was determined that the cycle would be broken. Maggie was to befriend her, talking with her on the phone, meeting with her as needed. They could attend meetings together at the office and perhaps become a support to one another. Maggie felt ready for the challenge, and could always use a little extra support herself. She agreed. The woman's name was Melody, and Sharon gave her Maggie's phone number.

Maggie enjoyed her first telephone conversation with Melody. She seemed like a wonderful woman, energetic and excited about her job as nanny to these young children. Maggie and Melody spent time "together" on the phone several times a week, learning to trust one another. They seemed to have much in common and enjoyed the sharing.

◆　　　◆　　　◆

Could Naomi Joy truly be two years old? Where did the last eighteen months go? She was such a cutie ~ and could she ever talk! Naomi Joy didn't start out with a lot of babbling like most children. After six months in America, hearing the English language, Naomi Joy started using sentences! At first, she would only string together two or three words, but it wasn't long before she was using clear and complete sentences. Such an extraordinary child! Her vocabulary at the age of two was absolutely remarkable.

She didn't enjoy a lot of the physical activities for which her brother showed such an aptitude. She didn't find pleasure in running, climbing, or jumping, but she loved games, puzzles, books, drawing, and coloring. Her mind seemed so quick, grasping concepts most two-year-olds were incapable of understanding. Maggie enjoyed "Table Time" with the children. It had always been enjoyable for her when Jason was small, and having Naomi Joy join in doubled the fun! They played Candyland, Chutes and Ladders, colored pictures, molded the play dough. The options were endless, and Naomi Joy seemed to love every one of them! Finger painting had to be the best, however.

Today, Maggie decided to try a "new" idea. The children didn't realize that the "finger paint" was left over frosting from a special surprise Maggie made for dessert. She gave each child a small bowl of "paint" and pieces of slick paper. The combination would be irresistible! Maggie sat down with the children, with her own bowl of "paint" and her own paper. They all chattered and painted, enjoying the texture of the paint on the paper. Naomi Joy made wide sweeping motions with her hands, delighted with the feel of the new paint. She drew a finger through the interesting design already covering her canvas, and noticed that she could draw pictures using just one finger. She made dainty, tiny design. Jason, on the other hand, kept using dramatic motions, sweeping paint across the page, running both hands through the paint. He had paint on his face, elbows, shirt…Maggie smiled at them. They were certainly entirely different in personality, tastes and interests!

Maggie looked at the mess on Jason and the clean little girl and laughed. Naomi Joy had come a long way since the day in the park last fall! She could finger paint, a messy project, now. Before she would have looked at that and refused to put her hands in it! They had taken advantage of Naomi Joy's obsession with food, and love for "Table Time", to help her learn to get messy. Meatloaf had to be mixed by hand (at THIS house, anyway!), bread had to be kneaded and finger paint had to be spread! Naomi Joy could finally get a little bit messy and deal with it!

Maggie remembered when Naomi Joy was first sitting up in her high chair at mealtime. Snooker saw the opportunity and laid in wait at the feet of the chair. Surely a tidbit or two would be coming down soon! Snooker waited in vain. Naomi Joy never dropped a snibble! It wasn't long before Snooker returned to his place under Jason's chair!

The children played in the paint for a long time before their attention began to wander. This was the moment Maggie had been awaiting. She said, "Well, it's time to clean up. Let's start with the paint…" She moved her hands up to her mouth and licked off some of the frosting.

Naomi Joy's eyes grew as round as saucers. Jason's mouth dropped open!

"Mmmm. So good!" Maggie watched their response as she licked the next finger. She pretended surprise. "Is something wrong?"

Naomi Joy continued to stare in shock and horror, while Jason said, "Mommy, you're eating *paint!*"

"No, no. Not paint! Try it yourself!"

Naomi Joy was the first to sample it, and a big grin broke out on her face. She urged her big brother to try it. Jason tasted it and laughed, "It's frosting!"

They all laughed ~ and "cleaned up" their projects!

That night, when Melody called, Maggie told her the story. They had a good laugh over it. "I wish we could always enjoy Naomi Joy so much. Some times she is such a delight ~ and I'm glad. Used to be that I *never* enjoyed her, but there are still so many times that I am so frustrated…"

"Well, maybe you don't spend <u>enough</u> time with her ~ maybe you need more times like that with her."

Maggie laughed. "Oh, I'm not so sure about that. Let me tell you our schedule. First we get up and fix breakfast together. We sit down and eat and then clean up together. Afterward, I take about thirty minutes to do something ~ clean house, make a phone call, do laundry. Then it is Table Time. We do a table activity like the painting or play a game. Then I take a break to finish up laundry or whatever. By then it is time to cook lunch. We eat and clean up together. After lunch, we take a walk and play at the park. Then it's "rest time" ~ Jason sleeps, and Naomi Joy cries. "Imagination Time" follows their naps when we play fireman or space people, or house or something. We make dinner for Daddy, eat, clean up, and after playing with Daddy for awhile, it's time for bed. I spend a lot of time with both children!"

"Well then, there's your problem! You simply give her too much attention!"

Maggie sighed. Everyone had an opinion, but nobody had any answers! Maggie changed the subject. At the end of their talk, Maggie told her that Naomi Joy and Jason would be joining her on a visit to see Sharon the following day. The children hadn't gone before, so playing in the play area at the office would be fun for them...

The Nightmare

The phone rang about mid morning. Adam had just started a new job in Colorado Springs. The job at the airline fizzled out and he spent only a short time looking before he found this new job. When the phone rang, Maggie wondered who it might be. Adam didn't normally call long distance, but it might be someone from the church. Melody always called in the evenings. Maggie picked up the phone.

"Maggie, this is Sally, from the agency."

"Yes, Sally, what can I do for you?"

Sally's voice was obviously strained when she answered, "We need to have a meeting here at the office this afternoon. We'll expect you at two o'clock ~ and bring Naomi Joy."

Maggie didn't understand. "What is this all about? What is going on?

"We'll talk about it more later. We'll plan on seeing you at two o'clock." Sally hung up.

Maggie was stunned. She'd never gotten a call like this before. What could it mean? Maggie looked up to the ceiling. "God what is this? What is happening?" And it came to her as a sudden, horrible revelation. They wanted Naomi Joy back. She didn't know why, but she knew, without a shadow of a doubt, that they wanted her back. All she could think was that the family was finally doing a little bit better ~ at least she could laugh now and then! Now, they wanted her little girl back!

Maggie started to cry again ~ like she hadn't cried in months! Her first thought was to call her friend from church. JoAnn was a mature Christian and had taken Maggie's family under her wing. She saw a family in need and she provided the encouragement they needed. JoAnn and Maggie had long conversations, shopped, laughed and had tea together. JoAnn adored Jason and Naomi Joy. She was the one to call now.

When JoAnn answered the phone, Maggie could hardly talk. She sobbed out as much of the story as she could. "JoAnn, the agency called. They want to take Naomi Joy! What am I going to do?"

JoAnn's response was immediate ~ and brief. "I'll be right there!"

Maggie tried to calm down as she waited for JoAnn. However, when she arrived twenty minutes later, Maggie was on the verge of hysteria. JoAnn simply walked over and wrapped her arms around Maggie, holding her until she cried herself to exhaustion. When she finally stopped, JoAnn handed Maggie a tissue and said, "Let's start at the beginning and tell me what you know."

Maggie told her what Sally said. JoAnn agreed that it did indeed sound like trouble ahead. She suggested that she call Adam down in Colorado Springs, ask him to come home for the emergency, and do whatever he said in the meantime. She stayed as Maggie put in the call. Adam told Maggie to call their lawyer immediately and that he would be home as quickly as possible.

John was their lawyer for this hoped for adoption. Maggie could not believe that the "baby" was now two years old and they were still fighting these ridiculous battles. John tried to calm Maggie down.

"Maggie, these people are personal friends of mine. I've known Sally for years! She would not deal with anyone in this fashion. I really do think you are over reacting. Naomi Joy is perfectly safe."

Maggie would not be swayed. "John, I hope you are right. But I have a feeling this is going to be a big deal. We want you there."

John was hesitant. "Maggie, I really think you will be wasting your money. Consider this carefully."

Maggie was trying to keep from moving back into hysteria. "It's our money and our baby, John. We need you there."

Obviously, there was no point in arguing. Maggie was set on having him there. He would meet Maggie, Adam and Naomi Joy at the agency.

Adam arrived from the Springs in just an hour and a half. He, Maggie and JoAnn discussed what they should do. It was decided that JoAnn would take Jason home with her. Adam, Maggie and Naomi Joy would go to the agency ~ after they had a time of prayer!

Maggie got Naomi Joy ready to go. They dressed her in the cutest outfit she had. She looked like a China doll ~ absolutely beautiful. There was still that rash ~ but what could be done about that? Maggie felt bad that it marred the baby's complexion.

John met Maggie and Adam in the parking lot of the agency. He repeated his opinion to Adam. Adam stood firm. Perhaps having John there was unnecessary, but Adam wanted him there anyway. John smiled indulgently and escorted the couple in.

Sally was waiting for them. Surprise registered on her face when she saw John there. He greeted her. "Hello, Sally. I am representing Maggie and Adam in this adoption process. They asked me to attend this meeting today."

Sally seemed to recover quickly. "Well, that isn't necessary, but you are welcome, none-the-less. Let's take Naomi Joy to the play area where she will meet some new friends. Are you ready, Naomi Joy?" Sally reached for the toddler who clung to her daddy, reluctant to let go. "I have a nice, big balloon waiting for you. You'd like a big balloon, wouldn't you?" With that wonderful prospect, Naomi Joy reached for Sally and allowed her to carry her to the playroom. Maggie watched with a feeling of dread closing its icy fingers around her stomach. She wondered if she would ever see that pretty little Korean face again. She felt the tears welling up and forced herself to think about other things. She would not, would *not* allow Sally to see any weakness in her!

When Sally returned, she escorted the small group to a meeting room where four other people were waiting. Maggie and Adam recognized none of them. Sally introduced each individual, but it had all become a blur to Maggie. She tried to smile. Sally invited the couple and their lawyer to have a seat.

Sally started the meeting. "We received a couple of reports that we would like to discuss with you. One is that you, Maggie, kicked Naomi Joy. The second is that you have been hitting her when she doesn't respond to you. We'd like to hear what you have to say in response."

Maggie looked at Adam, her eyes filled with pain and tears. She couldn't say anything. Adam took over, "Exactly what do you mean by this? You'll need to be more specific for us to know how to respond."

"Let's just start with the first allegation. The report *is* a bit more specific. The account came from your daughter. She said, 'My mommy kicked me out of the bathroom.'"

Maggie laughed. "Kicked her out of the bathroom! Is that all? And you think I actually <u>kicked</u> her!" She looked at the faces around the room. They showed absolutely no humor whatsoever. Apparently, they did indeed think she had kicked her toddler!

Maggie was taken aback. "Haven't you ever heard that expression? Being kicked out of a place? It doesn't mean actually being kicked..."

Her words obviously had no impact on the group. Sally spoke up. "Perhaps you would care to explain what happened?"

Maggie glanced at Adam again. He squeezed her hand under the table. Maggie could not believe this was really happening.

"Well, Naomi Joy followed me into the bathroom. I enjoy having privacy in the bathroom, so I <u>did</u> say, 'Sorry, I have to kick you out! Mommy's turn!', and I led her out of the bathroom and closed the door as I went back in."

Sally continued to look skeptical. "Are you *sure* that is what happened?"

"What do you mean, 'am I sure'? Of course I'm sure! I wouldn't actually *kick* Naomi Joy! It's simply an expression! Surely you've heard it before?!"

Sally glanced down at the papers in front of her. "The report uses the exact wording, using the word 'kicked'. Was anyone else present at the time?"

"Of course not! I rarely take an audience with me into the bathroom!" Maggie could feel Adam's hand tightening around her own.

John interrupted. Maggie was becoming upset enough she couldn't even process what he was saying. Adam moved his arm so that it surrounded her shoulders. He spoke soothingly to her. It was obvious that the meeting was far from over. She did need to get a grip on herself. She repeated her earlier resolution. She simply would <u>not</u> let this woman see her cry. As John and Sally and the others talked, she took several deep breaths and tried to relax.

"Maggie?" She looked up. Apparently, they had been addressing her and she'd missed it somehow.

"Yes?"

"The other allegation?"

Maggie tried to remember. "Other allegation? I'm sorry, I just can't remember what it was. Could you remind me?"

"The allegation is that you hit Naomi Joy when she didn't respond to you."

Maggie was mystified as to what this could possibly mean. "I'm sorry. I can't respond to that one ~ I don't know of any time that I've hit Naomi Joy because she didn't respond to me."

"You have no recollection of such an action?"

Maggie shook her head. "None at all."

Sally looked at Adam. "Maybe you can help us. When have you seen Maggie strike Naomi Joy?"

John interrupted again ~ something about leading questions.

Adam looked at Sally directly when he answered, "Maggie wouldn't hit Naomi Joy. I've never seen that happen."

The discussion became quite lively now. Everyone had questions or an opinion to state. All five of the people from the agency seemed to have strong feelings. John became heavily involved in the process as Adam and Maggie listened. Each of them had a few comments to make, but they seemed to have little, if any, impact. They grew more uncomfortable as the individuals began talking about them as if they weren't even there! John kept pulling to conversation back to the legal arena and the facts they had.

At one point, Adam asked where the accusations came from. It *is* a constitutional right to face ones accuser. However, in this kind of a situation, that constitutional right did not apply. Anonymity was vital in "Child Protection".

"How then, can we defend ourselves against them? You won't believe us, but you believe this 'anonymous person' without question? They have all the rights, and we have none?" Adam was also becoming frustrated with this whole process. Could this possibly even be *legal*?

"We received these allegations from a very respected and reliable source. There is no need to question it." Stated as a simple fact—no questions asked!

Maggie leaned over to her husband. "It's <u>got</u> to be Sharon and Melody. Who else would say this stuff? They might be considered a 'very respected and reliable source'."

Adam nodded grimly. Things were not looking good.

More discussion, more questions, more insinuations, more doubtful looks. It was pretty obvious that no one believed them, except John. He was standing with them, thank God. It seemed to go on and on and on. Maggie couldn't bear any more. No one believed her. They were all accusing her! What is the matter with the world anyway? Suddenly, she stood up. "Why can't any of you believe me? What is wrong with a mom wanting to be alone to pee? My God, I love Naomi Joy! What more can I do or say to prove it? What more do you want? Do I have to bleed for you to believe me? What is it you want from me?" Her voice had been escalating, but ended in a terrible sob. She just couldn't stand it all any more. She ran out of the room crying.

The room was absolutely silent with shock. The strength of Maggie's pain, her raw emotion hung heavy in the air. For several moments no one spoke. Adam looked toward the door, and John nodded. "Yes, you'd better go to her."

◆   ◆   ◆

Maggie was sitting on the stairs outside the room, crying uncontrollably. Adam never saw her so upset before this moment. He sat down quietly beside her and put his arm around her, saying nothing. When Maggie turned and clutched his shirt, he wrapped the other arm around her, cradling her in her pain. He said nothing, but simply rocked her as her violent weeping shook her whole body. When she calmed a bit, he handed her his handkerchief and let her wipe her eyes and nose. Still he said nothing.

Maggie's tear filled eyes sought his own. "What do they want from us, Adam? We've had her for over a year! How can we prove *anything* to them?"

Adam shrugged. "I don't think we can, Honey. They are believing what they choose to believe. We are going to have to trust John in this one. I don't know what else we <u>can</u> do. If God truly sent her to us, we have to keep trusting Him…" It sounded pretty lame, even to his own ears.

They sat together for awhile, Maggie trying to compose herself, Adam letting his thoughts roam over the events of the last year. It did look like he was losing his little princess, and there wasn't a thing he could see to do about it. Finally, as Maggie's sobs calmed to that funny little hiccuping that follows such an outpouring of emotion, he asked, "Ready to go back?"

"I **never** want to go back, Adam! I **never** want to see their faces again! What good would it do anyway?"

His voice lowered to a whisper. "We've <u>got</u> to go back, Honey. It may do no good at all, but we've got to see this through."

Maggie merely nodded. "Yes," she finally said.

As they entered the room, the talking stopped. Everyone looked at Adam, gently holding his shaken wife. He walked Maggie slowly to their chairs and helped her sit down. Maggie's eyes remained down, unwilling to make contact with anyone in the room. Two words seemed to barely escape from her lips. "I'm sorry." Adam's arm tightened around her shoulder, reassuring her.

It was a moment before anyone responded. Finally John spoke, "No apology needed, Maggie. This is very difficult. We all understand that. This is a terrible strain, but we may have come up with some suggestions…"

The talk began. The caseworker had obviously made a determination somehow that the problem was that Maggie must be Manic-Depressive and treatment for that was an absolute must. The Kemp Center had a qualified evaluator who could make the decision and recommend treatment. Naomi Joy would stay in the home, closely supervised, as Maggie followed through on the recommended treatment. With that, they were dismissed.

As John walked out with the couple, Naomi Joy carried by her determined father, Maggie apologized for her outburst again. John smiled. "You know, I think it was a good thing, in its own way. It was the turning point in the meeting. You were right, and I was wrong. They had every intention of taking Naomi Joy. But when they saw the emotion, the pain, the love and commitment you have for this little girl, the decision was changed. You may have to go through some difficult times ahead ~ but Naomi Joy will be going home with <u>you</u> and no one else! You owe no one an apology!"

Maggie shook her head. What a strange world…She had always thought love would be enough.

◆   ◆   ◆

The "assessment" at the Kemp Center suggested that Maggie would benefit from therapy. This came as no surprise to the family. Things had been discussed with the gentleman before he ever saw Maggie. He had a definite point of view before Maggie walked in the room and his "findings" merely confirmed that.

Things were somewhat complicated by the move to Colorado Springs for Adam's new job. It meant developing a new support group, getting yet another caseworker, and transferring all of the information to the Community Mental Health Center in the new city.

The new therapist was named Sarah, and Maggie liked her. They began with general information, and the caseworker's "diagnosis". Sarah listened to Maggie's story, the short history of Naomi Joy's life and behaviors, and started the formal assessment process. There were various tests and forms to be filled out ~ as honestly as possible, of course.

During the next six months, Sarah and Maggie began to develop a relationship, and Maggie found herself opening up more and more. She shared of her childhood, college years, marriage, her love for Jason and the excitement of finally having a son. She shared about the search for a daughter, and "finding" Naomi Joy. There were stories of Naomi Joy's homecoming and the painful health problems they had and continued to face. Sarah heard of the sleepless nights and unending crying, the two moves with Adam's jobs, and the horrible visit to the adoption facility where Maggie had broken down so badly.

Sarah seemed fair, honest, and open minded. She wasn't willing to look at things solely from Maggie's point of view, and talked with Adam as well. The recommendation from the agency was for Maggie to undergo treatment (at their own expense!) once a week for a minimum of one year. Sarah examined the results of the testing and the information she gathered over a six month period. A picture was taking shape, and she was becoming increasingly frustrated. Finally, after consulting with her team at the center, she approached Maggie with her plan. She called in both Maggie and Adam for a meeting.

"Adam, Maggie, I have been going over these test results, shared them with my team here at the Center, listened to both of you and watched you both with Naomi Joy over these past six months. I have to admit that I fail to see any reason to continue therapy. Maggie, I see a well adjusted, if stressed, individual, unusually bright, articulate, well informed and capable. You are both deeply committed to this child. I think our next step is to meet with the caseworker and discuss what to do. I can share my observations and recommend that we move on from here and get this child adopted!"

Adam and Maggie turned to each other with a shared smile. Finally, a ray of sunshine in a very dark situation. They heartily agreed to her plan.

The meeting was set for the following week. Adam and Maggie both attended this session and, after greeting Sally, introduced her to Sarah. Sarah shared her findings with the caseworker.

Sally looked surprised. "You see no indication of Manic Depressive behaviors?"

"None at all. I administered a number of tests, and they all indicated a healthy personality."

Sally pondered this response for several seconds. Then she asked, "Is there anyone else here that could evaluate the tests and find a Manic Depressive disorder?"

Sarah looked long and hard at the caseworker. "No, these tests are standard tests and are evaluated the same way by each professional. Ms. Avery, I note, even in our short time together, a marked hostility toward the Taylors. Perhaps you could tell me a little more about that?"

Maggie stifled a giggle and glanced at Adam who was covering a smile with his hand. His eyes twinkled, however, and Maggie could tell that he was thinking the same thing she was. Their therapist was psychoanalyzing their caseworker! This was absolutely delightful!

"Ms. Avery" and Sarah talked for some time, much to the amusement of the Taylors. There seemed to be no alternative for Sally other than acceptance of the results presented. Sally asked the therapist to provide a copy of her findings for the court and left. The report to the court would state, that in this professional's opinion, "the most detrimental factor in this child's life was the opinion of the caseworker and that opinion should be overridden and the Taylor's be allowed to adopt the child in question."!

On September 13, 1983, two years after her arrival into the United States of America, Naomi Joy was officially adopted into the Taylor family!

It was decided that there should definitely be a party to celebrate this great victory! Little Naomi Joy loved the popular cartoon character, Strawberry Shortcake and the gang that belonged with her. It would be perfectly natural, then, to decorate a cake in the shape and after the character of this favorite doll. She took Jason and Naomi Joy with her to the hobby store to pick up the cake pan and colors she would need. Naomi Joy was delighted with the idea of having a party, choosing her cake style, and setting up for the occasion. She took great care in her selection, finding exactly the right cake pan.

Naomi Joy's Sunday school teacher wanted to contribute to the occasion and decorated a second cake in keeping with the theme of the party. She and Maggie spent time together preparing for the event. It would be an open house. The adoption had been a long a difficult process, and many people had contributed to its completion.

Invitations were sent out, each with the quotation from I Samuel: "For this child I prayed, and the Lord has granted me my petition, which I made to Him." printed on the front. Indeed, much prayer had gone up to the Lord on behalf of this child! When Adam and Maggie found a plaque engraved with the quotation, they knew it was perfect and had carefully placed it in Naomi Joy's bedroom. If the cakes weren't already planned out, it would have been perfect to place it on each of them.

Maggie spent hours making just the right dress for the party. No lacy tights this time! But she would look like "Daddy's little princess" on this very special occasion. In no time, the day arrived, and everyone was ready. A veritable feast had been laid out! The cakes were so cute, and graced the center of the table. Naomi Joy loved them, and ran back and forth from the door, looking for guests, and the cakes, to give them one more check.

Adam had gone shopping with Maggie and they had placed a beautifully wrapped gift in the center of the gift table, surrounded by gay balloons of pink, red, and white. Soon the table was filled to overflowing with gifts for the little girl.

Naomi Joy was a perfect hostess and delighted everyone who walked in the door. She sat on laps, held hands, carried on amazing conversations for a child of two and a half, and entertained guests. The men were enchanted with her. The women admired her pretty new dress and manners. Jason, on the other hand, enjoyed playing with all the children that came, talking the boys into a game of football in the backyard.

When it finally came time to unwrap gifts, Naomi Joy was delighted to see that they were almost ALL for her! There was one or two for Jason, but the others were all hers! She exclaimed over each gift, much to the pleasure of the givers. Each one had to be carefully examined and shared with each person there. Naomi Joy made sure that every single person saw, and even touched, each prize.

When the little girl opened the gift from the pastor, Maggie and Adam gasped in surprise. It was a beautiful, wooden plaque, an oval over most of the surface covered with blue satin. Under the rising sun, beautifully embossed, was the same quotation from I Samuel, in full: "For this child I have prayed; And the Lord has granted me my petition, which I made to Him. Therefore I have lent him to the Lord; as long as he lives, He is lent to the Lord. (I Samuel 1:27-28)

Adam and Maggie glanced significantly at the pastor. Here, in Naomi Joy's hands, was their favorite gift of all! It would hang in a choice spot, displayed for all to see.

◆   ◆   ◆

Maggie thought that, with the adoption and all its complications behind them, things would finally settle down into a calmer, more sane pattern. Leaving behind the stress of "being under a microscope", as Adam put it, should have made a significant difference. Yet, when all the excitement was over and they tried to settle into a routine, Maggie found herself caught in the same old patterns. This home in Colorado Springs had the benefit of three floors. Maggie loved having an attic bedroom and bath, a floor all to themselves! The children were on the main floor. The distance meant that, for the first time since Naomi Joy had come to them Maggie could sleep every night. Somehow, the screaming did not bother Jason, across the hall from his sister; and he loved having his very own bathroom! Regular sleep had made much difference, but there were so many other problems.

Maggie had little trouble in the toilet training process with Jason. He hated being wet or dirty, and simply decided he wasn't going to do that any more. Not so with Naomi Joy. Maggie tried not to make an issue of it for that would only worsen the situation. But she strongly suspected that Naomi Joy was fully capable of this next step toward growing up. When it suited her, Naomi Joy would use the bathroom. When she was angry with Maggie, Naomi Joy would show her displeasure by having "accidents". These accidents were usually well timed, always at the most inconvenient time. Often they were strategically placed, in the most unpleasant of places! There can't be anything like opening the clothes hamper to do the laundry and finding a surprise hiding in there! Or on Maggie's favorite bedspread. Or her favorite pair of pants...

Maggie was also finding new possessions in Naomi Joy's room on an alarmingly regular basis. No matter how closely Adam and Maggie watched her, somehow Naomi Joy managed to come home from the store with a package of gum or a bit of candy. When returning from a visit to a friend's home, there was always the appearance of a new toy or two, as well as several handfuls of cereal, raisins or candy. It was useless trying to save chocolate chips for a special batch of cookies for Daddy, or animal crackers for a special snack time treat. Invariably, no matter when she hid them, when Maggie went looking for them, they would be gone. She stopped trying to convince herself that she had already used them and simply forgot.

The hoarding was interesting. Maggie could remember when Naomi Joy had to have food in both hands, and her mouth packed full…Now she kept little hordes of food in different places ~ only rarely her pockets! Maggie would find food under Naomi Joy's mattress, behind or under her dresser, in the corner of the closet, hidden in the very back of a drawer…It was always sweet or a starchy food ~ cereal, bread, potato chips, crackers. There seemed to be nothing that they could do to stop it ~ including providing a bowl of snacks, available throughout the day. The problem there, was that Maggie couldn't keep it supplied. As fast as anything went in, it disappeared, most likely to some corner in Naomi Joy's bedroom!

The difficult thing was that Naomi Joy never knew anything about the strange appearances of these things in her room. She denied having anything to do with their presence, although she didn't blame it on anyone else either. She simply had no idea how these things happened. She had started making up incredible but believable stories to account for some of them. It was very frustrating that others believed the tales, and there was no way Maggie could prove the stories one way or another.

◆   ◆   ◆

The new doctor seemed very kind. He was an older gentleman that must be someone's grandpa that read stories and went fishing with his grandchildren. He had been examining the rash that still covered Naomi Joy's body. Maggie had told him of all the different things they had tried to heal it up ~ creams, ointments, special soaps, special baths. Nothing had worked at all, and some of them made the problem worse!

The gentleman smiled. "These young doctors! They try all the new things and forget the old, faithful ones." He shook his head. "We are going to try an old fashioned remedy. I'll write a prescription for you. Go fill it, gently apply it twice a day, when Naomi Joy gets up and before she goes to bed. Don't put it on her face, I have something milder for her face. Give me a call in two weeks with your good report, okay?!"

Maggie was still skeptical, but this man inspired such confidence. It was like talking to her own father, whom she so sorely missed. She wanted to trust him, but these days, she could trust almost no one. Her feelings were so contrary to what they "should" be. Everyone loved Naomi Joy, and yet she couldn't do a single thing right. No matter what she tried, nothing worked; not on her skin, not in her behavior. But she would try this. Who knows?

Maggie was careful to follow the doctor's directions. Each day, she thought she noticed a change for the better. It was so gradual, but she was sure she was seeing improvement. She didn't want to hold her breath, but it did look hopeful!

It was just about two weeks later that Maggie realized that the house seemed awfully quiet. Jason was at a neighbor's house playing. But Naomi Joy was somewhere in the house.

Hmmm, where was she, and what was she doing? Maggie didn't have far to look. Naomi Joy was sitting in the rocking chair, gently rocking and running a hand over her little arm.

Maggie could hardly hear the words Naomi Joy was saying, but she did hear the wonder in her voice as Naomi Joy caressed her skin, saying, "Soft, so soft!"

Maggie sat down, tears in her eyes. Naomi Joy had never experienced "baby soft skin" before. Finally, Naomi Joy wasn't hurting!

◆   ◆   ◆

Maggie still couldn't believe that Naomi Joy, with the ear infections cleared up, her skin soft and pretty (except when she stole and ate too much sugar ~ this seemed to cause it to flare up again!), the adoption complete, and time behind them settling into a regular routine, still hadn't really done a lot better.

The crying and screaming every night continued. Bonnets and mittens no longer kept her from scratching herself, of course. However, the clearing of her skin definitely helped, thank God! A most amazing thing had happened. One night, the screaming even got to Adam, who seldom reacted to it. This time, notwithstanding his high tolerance level, he was unusually tired. He went into the bedroom and looked at Naomi Joy as she screamed. He tried several things ~ singing, patting her back, rubbing her back, murmuring his love to her ~ and found them unsuccessful. In frustration, he picked her up and gave her a quick swat over her diaper. Naomi Joy looked at him in surprise, closed her eyes and went limp as she fell asleep.

Adam returned to their own bedroom in amazement. "You won't believe what worked, Maggie!" He related the story to Maggie, puzzled. "Why did that work, and work so immediately? She just went limp in my arms, and was asleep. Why?"

Adam and Maggie puzzled over it for some time. Adam wondered, "Is it possible that, now the ear infections and skin infections are healed up, she can't sleep? Was she so accustomed to the pain, that it became 'normal'? Now she can't sleep because she doesn't hurt?"

Maggie was also perplexed. Naomi Joy didn't respond much to pain any more. As she thought about this event, she remembered another that was shocking to her at the time.

Naomi Joy had been playing in the back yard with Jason. They were playing happily, but became thirsty. Naomi Joy came in for a drink. When she approached Maggie, Maggie gasped. There was blood trickling down the side of Naomi Joy's face, and over her round little cheek.

"What happened, Naomi Joy? How did you hurt your head?"

Naomi Joy looked surprised. She reached up to her face, then looked down at her blood-smeared hand. Her surprise was obvious. "Don't know."

Adam and Maggie had been encouraging Naomi Joy to tell them when she had an "owie". They went out and bought special "Naomi Joy" Band-Aids. They told her, that if she ever saw blood, she could come to either one of them and get one of her special, cartoon Band-Aids. They had encouraged Jason to watch as well ~ if his little sister was "hurt", he could bring her to his parents, so they could treat the problem.

Not long after this, when Naomi Joy was playing on the floor with Jason, Maggie went over to give her a big hug. Maggie was trying hard to "catch Naomi Joy being wonderful', and reinforce whatever the behavior might be with a hug, sticker, handful of Cheerios, or just about anything else that seemed to work. When she picked up Naomi Joy, Maggie almost dropped her. Naomi Joy was HOT! She was burning up with fever!

Maggie ran for the thermometer. She was absolutely amazed when she read the results ~ Naomi Joy had a fever of 105°! How could this be? She had shown no symptoms at all! And she had a fever of 105°! Maggie called the doctor and made an appointment. As she waited for time to go, she ran a lukewarm bath and bathed the struggling child. Naomi Joy wanted to go play, but Maggie knew she had to get that fever down, if she could.

When the doctor examined the child, he, too, was astonished. "You say she showed no symptoms? She didn't complain at all?" Maggie shook her head. "This child has double ear infections and a severe step throat."

As the doctor questioned Naomi Joy, and wrote out the prescription for her, he considered this strange situation. He, too, had noticed that she rarely reacted when she had to have shots or other procedures done that usually drew a tear or two from other children. He tested his theory.

"Maggie, Naomi Joy *does* seem to *feel* pain. Evidently, she has learned to ignore it somehow. It isn't that unusual in some children. What is unusual is for her to be able to block such intense pain. You must be very vigilant with Naomi Joy ~ watch her closely. She could easily jeopardize her own safety."

Maggie responded, but did not say, "So, what else is new?", as she was tempted to do!

Maggie told Adam all of this. They watched Naomi Joy over the course of the next few days, taking her temperature several times each day. It stayed high, even though it didn't seem to bother Naomi Joy at all. The kept in constant touch with the doctor, and visited his office twice more ~ each time with the fever still hovering around 105°! At the end of the last phone call, the doctor told them that they would continue the Tylenol, cool baths, antibiotics, etc. for the evening. If the fever was still high in the morning, Naomi Joy would have to be hospitalized.

Adam called the church prayer chain and put Naomi Joy on it. The thought of hospitalization was frightening to him.

In the morning, Adam arose and went right into his little girl's bedroom. Naomi Joy smiled at her daddy and reached for him. Adam was jubilant as he carried his precious daughter into his bedroom. "The fever has broken, Maggie! She is as cool as a cucumber!"

It seemed miraculous to Adam and Maggie. Naomi Joy had run a temperature of 105° for five days ~ not to be broken until they finally remembered to pray! Adam pondered this ~ why did they so consistently forget this important factor? How could they raise Naomi Joy without it?

In spite of the calmer life style that the family was finally able to adopt, Naomi Joy's frequent temper tantrums continue to escalate. Not only did they escalate in terms of volume level; they increased in the level of violence. Maggie never ceased to be amazed at the intensity of these episodes. Naomi Joy was willing to lash out at anyone nearby when she was angry. She would destroy everything within her reach. And she seemed so extraordinarily strong!

Maggie tried to glean suggestions from the "seasoned" moms around her. She read books, and tried to draw from her teaching experience. Yet nothing seemed to equip her for this kind of tantrum, and nothing seemed effective in calming her daughter.

Many advisors suggested isolating Naomi Joy for the duration of the tantrum ~ either in her room or time out. She would be able to leave time out when she was calmer and better able to cope with life around her. Yet, when isolated, Naomi Joy could scream for a solid two or three hours with no sign of let up. Maggie couldn't allow it to continue on; remembering the countless hours of screaming they had endured when the child was smaller. Staying in time out was impossible ~ Naomi Joy would lash about, destruction inflicted all around her.

Maggie tried holding Naomi Joy in her time out ~ but was unable to maintain her hold over the child. The strength she exhibited was unbelievable. And the voices scared Maggie…

The voices! What a strange thing! There were times, in her anger, that Naomi Joy spoke in voices Maggie did not recognize. Sometimes there were words that a three or four year old could not possibly know, pronounced perfectly. Sometimes the voice was harsh, deep, like a man's. Other times, it was high, a shriek that seemed to emit from deep within her ~ or from another world. There was the animal like, deep growl. It was eerie, scary. Maggie hated hearing them…She tried to describe them to Adam, but he couldn't understand what she was talking about. Another one of those areas Maggie wondered if she wasn't simply going crazy…

There was no denying the strength Naomi Joy could display. The time that, in her rage, Naomi Joy simply tore her bedroom door off its hinges was undeniable! The evidence was quite clear and shocked Adam when he came home. He didn't want to believe the story, but Jason confirmed it, and Naomi Joy refused to talk about it.

Adam and Maggie had approached their pastor about it ~ but it was dismissed as a story. After all, he knew sweet little Naomi Joy, and she never acted in such a manner that he had ever seen! Often Maggie questioned her own sanity and even Adam had to wonder on occasion!

Another odd thing was Naomi Joy's ability to "read" other people. Maggie and Adam had watched in amazement when they had held a gathering in their home. As each person entered, Naomi Joy was the perfect hostess. If the person was not one that particularly enjoyed young children, Naomi Joy greeted them respectfully and with great dignity, "Please come in. May I take your coat? Please join us upstairs…"

If the adult was very child oriented, Naomi Joy was the typical little girl. She giggled, responded to being "chucked" under the chin, loved to be tickled, and was so charming. For each individual, Naomi Joy was able to completely change personality. What was this? They had never seen such behavior in a child before. It was more than either Adam or Maggie could explain. Strange, though, that other people didn't notice it.

Naomi Joy's intellect was astounding. Adam and Maggie decided to order a set of encyclopedias that would come one or two volumes at a time. At the age of four, Naomi Joy looked forward to the arrival of the volumes with great anticipation! She would speculate what she would find in each. "E is for elephant! And Eskimo! I wonder what we will learn about them?" When they would arrive, Naomi Joy would spend hours pouring over the pictures, tracing the words on the page. She would beg Maggie to read to her and sit enraptured as she drank in every word. They encyclopedias became her favorite reading materials!

The day came when Adam made the announcement, "It is time for this family to get a computer." It was true ~ it would challenge Naomi Joy and Jason would love it as well. It was time for Maggie to learn to use one as well. So, the computer came into the Taylor home.

Maggie loved the new computer. At first, it took some getting used to. Later, Maggie would send out about thirty-five letters a month on the word processor. And she loved playing "Frogger"! Adam and Maggie bought some pre-reading games for the children. Jason was starting on the big adventure of reading, and it was obvious that Naomi Joy would soon be following, in spite of the three year age difference.

Jason loved the games that included mazes. He loved traveling through the mazes to capture whatever it was he was supposed to secure! It was great fun to see if he could beat Mom or Naomi Joy to the goal. It wasn't long before he was able to race through the games at such a rate of speed; neither could keep up with him!

Naomi Joy preferred a less complicated game. In hers, a letter, part of a word, or picture would descend from the top of the screen. When she pressed the corresponding letter on the keyboard, the object would explode. What great fun! One day, Maggie heard Naomi Joy crying in frustration as she played her game. She went to see what the problem was, since Jason was in school now and unavailable to help his little sister.

"What's wrong, Naomi Joy?" Maggie studied the screen. A little picture of a rabbit was coming down, so Naomi Joy was supposed to push the "r" on her keyboard. Simple enough.

"It's 'w', Mommy. I know it's a wabbit, but it won't take the 'w'!" Naomi Joy answered in such a pathetic little voice.

"Oh!" chuckled Maggie. "It is a 'wabbit', honey. But most people say 'rabbit' so you are supposed to push the 'r', not the 'w'!"

Naomi Joy quickly pushed the "r". To her amazement, the picture exploded with a satisfying noise. "Hmm, wabbit starts with 'r'…" she murmured as Maggie returned to her sink full of dirty dishes, quietly laughing to herself. She'd have to remember this one for Adam!

◆   ◆   ◆

After much discussion, Adam and Maggie agreed it was time to take Naomi Joy in for an evaluation. They had tried to get help for her, to see it they could find some answers as to how to deal with such an unusual child. No one seemed to understand that Naomi Joy was in trouble. The tantrums continued, and worsened. She continued to tear at her own flesh, inflicting terrible wounds. There were more episodes of "the voices" and great destruction. Naomi Joy seemed to enjoy time with her Daddy, but showed absolutely no affection toward her mother. Maggie was the target of great fury, often for no apparent reason. Naomi Joy was still unable to sleep at night and had taken to wandering through the house at night. Adam and Maggie tried to teach Naomi Joy to stay in her bedroom rather than wandering the house, taking food and hiding it, breaking Maggie's possessions, or taking and hiding Jason's toys.

It was particularly unnerving one night. Maggie awoke with a start, aware that something was not right in the bedroom. She held her breath and listened. Nothing. What had awakened her? Quietly, so as not to wake up Adam, she whispered, "Naomi Joy?"

"Yes?" came a voice out of the dark, next to the bed.

"Are you ready to go to bed now?" asked Maggie.

There was silence for a moment and then came her daughter's answer. "Okay."

After Naomi Joy left the room, Maggie shivered. She wondered how long Naomi Joy had stood there in the dark, watching them sleep? What was she looking for? What did she want? What was she thinking? Maggie had a difficult time going back to sleep…

Every time they went for help, from the church, therapists, even the Department of Human Services, they were told that the problem was rooted in the marriage relationship, not the child. Naomi Joy was, of course, simply a child of four. How could any of these things be true? They must be imagined, particularly on Maggie's part. It was Maggie, not Naomi Joy that needed help. If she underwent some therapy, and together Adam and Maggie went to marriage counseling, things would work out! Yet, the more marriage counseling they received, the worse Naomi Joy's behaviors! It was almost as if she was trying to split the marriage apart! But surely not…

Over the last four years, Adam and Maggie had received countless hours of "help" and spent hundreds of dollars ~ yet no change for the better seemed to occur! However, now they had a new name, and maybe a new hope.

Naomi Joy spent several hours with the new therapist, Stuart. He called her parents in for a meeting to discuss his findings. "You do not have a disturbed youngster here. You have an extremely *gifted*, disturbed youngster! That is <u>much</u> more difficult to deal with!"

"Oh, this is helpful! Thank you for the encouragement", thought Adam. "So what now?" he asked out loud.

Stuart explained the tests he had administered, including an I.Q. test. "She tested off the scale. I could not get a reading on her, because she exceeded the limits for a child of her age! She doesn't have the skills to express much of what she knows!"

They worked with Stuart for some time, but there was only so much he could do. He told them that they were doing the right things, and he realized that it was frustrating to continue doing the "right things" and see no results. But they must not give up. There was a future for this child, and the only way she would get there was if the parents remained consistent and faithful to her. Consistency, stability, predictability, consequences, a consistent schedule, stimulation and challenge, all these things were needed. Keep on doing what you're doing and don't give up in spite of the lack of results.

Maggie broke down. "I just can't keep at it, Adam. I feel like I am worthless as a mother and a failure as a wife. Naomi Joy would be better of in the zoo with a monkey for a mother rather than me!"

Adam held his weeping wife. What could he do? What could he say? Were there any answers?

Adam and Maggie talked long into the night. It was time for Maggie to find some outlet that gave her a sense of satisfaction and fulfillment. It was time for her to get out and away from home for awhile each day. It was decided that it was time for Maggie to go back to teaching.

Maggie was excited to get back into the classroom again. She was willing to volunteer at the deaf school, since getting a paid position in the middle of the school year is difficult. She requested the lowest level classroom available. She loved teaching preschool and kindergarten! While she waited for a response she tried to practice her sign language skills. The years of being a stay at home mom and made her skills a bit rusty. Hopefully she would get a hearing teacher and break back into it slowly!

Maggie's assignment was the first grade classroom ~ with a deaf teacher! Maggie laughed. Well, if God wanted her back in these classrooms, perhaps it was for the best! She absolutely loved Lanai! She was an older lady, very experienced and possessing the wisdom that comes of that experience. The children in the classroom adored Mrs. Lanai and responded so well to her. Maggie quickly felt at home and kept busy, working with the students. It was a joy to be back with the children!

Maggie was able to drop Jason off at school, drop Naomi Joy off at the baby sitters, and get to the school early on her three days a week she volunteered. Patty was so good to take Naomi Joy, and delighted to do so. She had been Naomi Joy's Sunday School teacher for awhile, and found Naomi Joy to be such a delight. Patty's husband was on a "remote" with the service, and the children enjoyed playing with the little one. Things started out so smoothly, and Maggie thought perhaps that they had hit on the answer. Adam was a wise man! All she needed was some time out, with other people. It made the week go so much smoother and gradually Maggie began to feel more like her old self! Maybe Polly-Anna was not dead after all!

It wasn't long before Maggie met another teacher, from the high school, that was waiting for the arrival of two young children from Korea. Maggie made a point of meeting Myra and talking to her about the expectations and excitement of waiting for these two boys. They were a little bit old, so would come to Myra and her husband speaking the language and ready to run around and explore this new country. Maggie found herself being almost optimistic about the arrival and that, with love, almost any situation can be overcome. Maggie was almost as excited as Myra when word arrived that the boys would be arriving in a couple of weeks. Myra would be taking maternity leave ~ Maggie would be filling in for her.

There were only two or three months left in the school year ~ surely I can handle high school for that short a season, thought Maggie. This was definitely NOT her area of interest, but maybe the experience would be good for her.

Now, it became even more important for Maggie to be up on time, get Jason ready to send off to school and Naomi Joy ready for day care. Naomi Joy was finding it more and more amusing to be as difficult as possible in the mornings, refusing to get dressed, refusing to be ready to get in the car…Finally, Maggie told her that, if she refused to get dressed, Maggie would wrap her up in a towel and take her to day care naked!

Maggie never ceased to be amazed how every consequence she came up with, Naomi Joy found a way around it, to make it more a frustration for Mom than a consequence for herself. Naomi Joy loved going to the day care naked ~ when she arrived the two older girls delighted in taking her into the bathroom and dressing her! Good grief! Even when Maggie made it clear that this was not supposed to be a pleasant consequence, it was just too much of a temptation for the girls to resist. Naomi Joy would somehow convince them that she was helpless and really did need "help" getting dressed. And who could resist those gorgeous brown eyes? Maggie decided that it just wasn't worth it. Let them do as they would and she would just go to work and enjoy not having to worry about it.

High school was just as challenging as Maggie had expected, and maybe even more so. Never in her wildest dreams would she think that one of her students would assault another student on his way to Maggie's class, sending the girl that just broke up with him to the hospital! And who would believe that another student would actually pick Maggie up deposit her into the hall outside the classroom door, lock it and ransack the room? Such destruction! Maggie had never seen anything like it! Maggie was so grateful with another teacher became available to take the afternoon classes off her hands. A half-day of school would go a long way in reducing the stress and helping her be available for other, more pleasant work. Her heart would always be with the "little ones". She would be much wiser about taking high school students ever again! Her respect for Myra rose with every day that passed!

Patty met Maggie at church one Sunday, as the school year was drawing to a close. "You know, Maggie, I used to think you were over exaggerating when you talked about the problems with Naomi Joy. I pretended to be sympathetic, but Naomi Joy seemed like such a wonderful child..." Patty paused, and seem to gather her thoughts. "I own you an apology. I know now the stories are true...I'm sorry."

Maggie was dumbfounded. Never had anyone acknowledged that maybe it wasn't all Maggie's problem! She wasn't sure what to say! "Well, Patty, what in the world happened?"

"Well, I haven't mentioned it before because I knew how stressed you were. But she has been doing...things..."

Maggie waited expectantly. Then she urged Patty on. "Like what things?"

Patty was sorting information. "Well, like the Cheerios and stuff in the closet. I was cleaning out my youngest daughter's closet, and there was what you call a 'stockpile' of cereal and pop tarts ~ stuff like that. I asked her about it, and she hadn't realized it was there! I started looking around, and lots of stuff is missing. It is mostly food, a little bit of makeup, jewelry, a few toys ~ nothing real big. And there are little stockpiles all over the house that I am finding. Only the food is there, not the other stuff…"

"I can look for the other stuff. Maybe I'll find it in her stockpiles at home." answered Maggie.

"It doesn't matter, Maggie. Anyway, I put it all together when I found Naomi Joy going through the *trash!* Maggie, she's been eating my *garbage!* I swear, Maggie, I had no idea! I can't imagine why she isn't sick! I am so sorry…Then I realized that is where the toothpaste went, too! And…"

Maggie touched her friend's shoulder. "It's okay, Patty. Don't tell me any more. Believe me ~ I understand! Last week, Naomi Joy asked her daddy if she could eat the 'strawberries' out in the grass in the backyard. Adam was confused and asked her to show him what she meant. She took him out and showed her a spot where the dog had vomited…

Patty shook her head. "I just can't believe it! Even seeing it, I couldn't believe it…"

Maggie smiled, all be it, a sad smile. Well, maybe she wasn't crazy after all! Small consolation, but it was some encouragement that another person was finally seeing some of this strange "stuff"!

◆   ◆   ◆

As the end of the school year, Maggie and Adam agreed that it was very likely time for Maggie to go back to work full time. She put in her application at the deaf school and at another school, that would be starting up in the fall. It was a brand new Christian school, backed by a total of six of the area "charismatic" churches. It would be with hearing children, but at least she wouldn't have to teach high school!

One of the biggest obstacles would be day care. Naomi Joy needed more challenge, more stimulation. She was showing more and more giftedness and would need a strong learning environment for this last year before she started kindergarten. Patty had also gracefully declined the job for some reason!

Maggie was excited when the new Christian school asked her if she would please come in for an interview. It went well and before long, the awaited call came. She got the job! Maggie asked what grade they needed her to teach. She was thrilled when she found out that she was at the top of the list and could choose her position. There was no question but that she wanted the kindergarten position ~ what else was there?! Kindergarten is full of excited children, eager children whose curiosity and inquisitiveness had not yet been quenched by years of schooling! What a joy and delight. The question that kept her awake at night was, how different would it be working with children that can actually hear???!!!

Adam and Maggie explored a number of possibilities for childcare. They found a licensed daycare that looked like it might be great for Naomi Joy. There would be plenty of educational opportunities, structured learning times and activities, unstructured "free play", supervision at all times, a big playground, enough other children in the class to give her plenty of social interaction, and a program that she could attend part time for the gifted and talented. It was a perfect place! Adam and Maggie were excited about it, Naomi Joy could hardly wait to start, and Jason would be going with Mom every day for school. It looked like an ideal arrangement.

Maggie had to get Naomi Joy up early each day. She needed a bath every morning after sleeping in a wet bed. That continued until after she turned eight years old. Naomi Joy was able to tell Maggie if she would be wet or dry each night. If she felt like it, she would stay dry, but if she was angry, or had her feelings hurt, felt like she was still hungry, she would be wet. Most of the time, she didn't feel like being dry ~ so she wasn't!

It did not end until that day Maggie took her in for a professional hair cut and styling as a reward for some outstanding behavior. Afterwards, Naomi Joy walked around, "puffing" her hair, saying, "I am a big girl now. I don't need to wet my bed anymore." And sure enough, after that haircut, she never wet her bed again!

It wasn't long before Maggie knew she was exactly where she needed to be! She loved "her" children, being in the classroom, associating with professional friends and sharing encouragement with parents. She received so much in return. The children responded to Maggie's enthusiasm with their own, touching Maggie's heart as it had not been touched in a long, long time! She had been concerned that her heart had grown so cold and hard that she would never enjoy working with children again, even in the professional setting. Yet, here she blossomed, reaching out and impacting these young lives. There was such laughter, such joy! Maggie looked forward to Mondays in a way she had long ago forgotten. Each Friday, she shared the bad news with the children in her classroom, that for two whole days, they wouldn't have class. But then, Monday would come and they would be together again. They played games on the playground, shared secrets, prayed together, learned to read, encouraged one another and hugged one another. Maggie worked well with the parents, and became friends with many of them. After four years of such pain, Maggie found contentment. She remained in this school for four, wonderful years.

Naomi Joy, on the other hand, did not fare so well. During that first year of preschool she was moved four times. It seemed that Maggie was not the only one who struggled in the caretaker role for this bright little girl. The learning environment was one in which Naomi Joy would truly shine, but her many of her behaviors were simply not acceptable in larger groups of children. It was difficult to develop any relationships, because other children learned to guard themselves from the trouble Naomi Joy brought.

Adam had to take Naomi Joy to school, pick her up afterward, and interact with the staff. He understood that Maggie could no longer cope with the complaints and concerns of people who could not possibly understand Naomi Joy, and who usually placed the blame on the child's mother. She felt guilty enough, without trying to cope with the criticism of others, no matter how qualified those people seemed to be to make judgments concerning her family!

It was difficult for Adam as well, however. He was frequently called in for the most bizarre problems! Maggie often helped him find the humor in each situation, making it easier to bear. When the teachers complained about Naomi Joy crawling around on the floor, licking the carpet after lunch and art, Maggie laughed and asked why they weren't getting paid for what the staff saved in cleaning fees! Besides that, who can blame a child for wanting a varied diet? A little glue and glitter would dress up any meal!

The same question should apply to the bathroom cleaning. When Naomi Joy "cleaned up" whatever she found in the bathroom (no matter how revolting to the rest of us!), why didn't that get deducted from their tuition? Naomi Joy, for dessert, ate the paper towels. She had a definite preference for the brown over the white...

But even Maggie had difficulty finding something to laugh about when the staff complained about Naomi Joy going through all the lunch boxes, and consuming the other children's lunches. Often, Naomi Joy would hoard the food in different hiding places. Always, she made sure her own stomach was satisfied. It was amazing the amount of food that she could eat! When questioned, if she chose to tell the truth, Naomi Joy would answer that she took the food because she wanted it. The feelings of the other children had no bearing on her behavior. Naomi Joy's concern was strictly personal. If she wanted it, she took it. If Adam could return the item, he would, but when it came to food, how could he make up for it? No consequence the staff and family tried seemed to affect Naomi Joy.

Her personal philosophy seemed to be "If I want it, it's mine"! As Naomi matured, the stealing became more and more subtle. She was rarely caught. When she was, store managers, school administrators, and even law enforcement personnel seemed so charmed by her that they rarely brought consequences to bear...

Maggie and Adam looked forward to the time when they could put Naomi Joy into the private school where Maggie was working. Jason seemed to enjoy it. With both Maggie and Jason there, their hope was that it would be easier to structure Naomi Joy's day so that behavior would change. She could go into Maggie's classroom, where Maggie worked with her and help her. But, as spring approached and Naomi Joy had to leave the third day care center, they both wondered if they would make it to the next fall! Adam and Maggie found a friend who was willing to watch the child. Perhaps going back to a one-on-one situation would help, at least for these last few months...

Each time Maggie felt frustrated with Naomi Joy, the clever child would do something to make her mother laugh. One evening, when it was Naomi Joy's turn to set the table for dinner, Maggie watched. Naomi Joy selected two of her brother's favorite drinking cups. Both were cute, with cartoon characters. Both cups were favored by <u>both</u> children. It was obvious that Naomi Joy wanted the Pooh Bear cup. She carefully placed it above her own plate, and the Rabbit one at her brother's place. She looked at the settings and, much to Maggie's surprise, switched the two cups, taking the second favorite cup for herself. It wasn't long before Maggie's curiosity at this was satisfied.

Maggie called Jason and Adam to dinner. As soon as Jason walked into the dining room, he glanced at Naomi Joy's place setting. Sure enough, Naomi Joy had the gall to place one of his favorite cups at her own place!

Without even a glance at his own setting, he turned to his sister, glaring, hands on his hips. "Naomi, you know that is my cup. What is it doing at *your* place???!!!"

Without missing a beat, Naomi Joy said, "Oh, Jason, I'm sorry. Did you want the Rabbit cup?" With exaggerated kindness she took the Pooh Bear cup from his place, and switched it with the Rabbit one at hers, gracefully getting what <u>she</u> wanted in the first place. She smiled sweetly at her older, somewhat confused, brother.

He glanced at both places, realizing that <u>he</u> was the one that had lost out, but what could he say? He had gotten exactly what he asked for, but realized that he had been greatly manipulated! Naomi Joy had neatly tricked him out of that!

◆   ◆   ◆

Maggie and Adam signed up for the coming retreat with the church. It was always such fun to go to the mountains, and to do so with these special people would make it a time to remember for a long, long while. There would be opportunity for renewal and encouragement, and the timing could not be better. They prepared Jason and Naomi Joy for the event as well. This would be a family retreat, with activities for the whole family! The children enthusiastically prepared their little backpacks, including their Bibles and outside, "play in the mountains" clothes!

The weekend was perfect. There was a room for the girls, a room for the boys, and rooms for the couples. The families played games, went exploring, fished, shared meals with the group, spent time praying and studying, and enjoyed the fun and company of one another.

After dinner the last evening, the adults put the children to bed, tucked them in, passed out the necessary hugs, kisses and drinks of water. Then they gathered together for a final evening of board games and talk. Many were the jokes and funny stories of parenting and there was much laughter.

Suddenly, one of the older girls appeared from the girls' room. "Naomi Joy fell off her bed."

Maggie knew it would happen. The child insisted on sleeping on the top bunk. They did put up the railing and even put some pillows there to protect her. Maggie knew, somehow, it would happen.

Adam rose, and checked on the child. Maggie followed behind. When they arrived on the scene, little Naomi Joy was laying on the floor, still asleep. Adam gently picked her up, and at Maggie's urging, placed her on the nearby bottom bunk bed. Naomi Joy never awakened. And why should they be surprised? Naomi Joy had shown such a tolerance for pain, and it wasn't unusual to find her sleeping in odd places. Her night wanderings often took her into places one doesn't normally sleep. Adam kissed the child's forehead and the couple left the room.

The next morning, Naomi Joy slept in late and needed to be awakened. She was still so sleepy. Evidently the excitement of being with so many other people, change in schedule, staying up late and all the play had taken its toll! Maggie wasn't too concerned until breakfast call came, and Naomi Joy didn't feel like eating. This was unheard of! Naomi Joy not wanting to eat? This was a new expe-rience. Maggie felt the child's forehead, but she didn't seem unusually warm. She looked into the deep, deep, black eyes. Naomi Joy's eyes were so dark, you couldn't tell the pupil from the iris. She smiled, remembering the time Naomi Joy had hit her head and they had been checking for a concussion by looking to see if her eyes were dilated. What a joke that was!!

"Well, Naomi Joy, why don't you just sit here and rest and we'll see if you feel up to something a little later." Naomi Joy nodded and rested her head on the chair back. Maggie mentioned the unusual behavior to Adam and they agreed that they would keep a close eye on the moppet…

Saying good-bye to everyone that morning was difficult. Of course, they would see these people again, each Sunday, and at other meetings, but the feeling of camaraderie, the closeness, would be lost as time went on. The problem with "mountain top experiences" is that one always must return to the valley.

Naomi Joy remained listless. Adam and Maggie tucked her in her seat belt, handed her the teddy bear she loved so dearly, and encouraged her to rest. On their way back to Colorado Springs, they planned on stopping at Adam's brother's home for dinner and to spend time with him and his wife. They rarely got together, so everyone was looking forward to the time there.

"Mommy, Naomi Joy is going to be sick!" came the warning from the back seat. Adam pulled the car over to the side of the road. Jason's voice became dis-gusted, "GROSS! She just threw up all over the place!"

Maggie got out of the car and went around to the passenger seat behind Adam. Naomi Joy was indeed sick, and her teddy bear would never be the same again either. She quickly unbuckled her daughter and got her out of the car. Naomi Joy continued to retch until her little tummy couldn't possibly have any-thing else in it. Adam took over with Naomi Joy while Maggie got out the towels and wipe ups and began mopping up the car and teddy bear. Jason helped by ending his vivid description of events and going to play in the grass near by.

When things were restored as well as could be expected, the family got back into the car and continued on down to Denver. Adam asked Naomi Joy if she felt better, and up to the visit, or should they just go home and let her rest. Naomi Joy wanted to see her aunt and uncle.

Kurt and Renee where delighted to see the family pull up. They greeted one another and entered the home together, including the two big dogs. The dinner table was set up and the house smelled wonderful! Renee was busy putting the last touches on a magnificent meal when Jason came into the kitchen.

"She's doing it again, Mom." he stated in a strained voice.

Maggie didn't have to ask what "it" was, but went into the bathroom to help Naomi Joy, telling Jason to get his dad.

Maggie was worried about Naomi Joy. "Adam, something is really wrong here. There's no fever at all, and she hasn't eaten hardly anything. But she is so sick. I hate to ask, when we never come here to visit, but I think we'd better get her to the hospital…"

Adam grimly agreed. "I'll talk to Kurt and get clearance from the insurance company…"

While Adam was on the telephone, trying to get things arranged, Maggie apologized to Renee. "I'm so sorry. I feel so badly. But, she really is doing badly."

Renee, always gracious, understood, and sat with Maggie as they encouraged the little one to rest. Hopefully, they could get her to a hospital here in Denver, rather than driving all the way down to the Springs with the sick child.

It was not to be. The insurance company would not clear them for a nearby facility. Adam had to bundle up the children and they continued their trip back to the Springs and the hospital where Naomi Joy could be seen.

The news there wasn't good. The doctor carefully examined Naomi Joy and asked questions. He shined his light in the child's eyes, first one and then the other. Maggie knew exactly what he meant when he said, "Well, we'll have to look at the *other* signs…" At least she wasn't the *only* one who couldn't see pupils in those big eyes!

As the doctor examined Naomi Joy, he explained to the parents what he was finding. It was in private that he told them the baby's concussion was severe, there might be bleeding in the brain, and surgery was a strong possibility. He would be keeping her under observation for "a bit".

Adam went to the telephone. He called the pastor, explaining the situation. Pastor put the need immediately on the church's prayer chain. They knew that getting as many people praying as possible was vital. As each individual contacted called the next on the prayer chain, it wasn't long before the whole church was involved in lifting Naomi Joy up to God. It wasn't long before the doctor pulled them aside again. "Naomi Joy is responding to the treatment much better. We won't be needing the surgery. I think we can release her in just a little while, but here are some instructions I want you to follow." He outlined what they were to watch for in Naomi Joy's behavior and responses, and told them it was important to awaken her every couple of hours and ask her a question or two to determine her coherence. It wasn't long before the couple was able to return home with Jason and Naomi Joy, well on the way to recovery!

Adam pondered the events of the previous evening. "You know, Maggie, when Naomi Joy didn't wake up after that fall from the bunk, do you think she could have actually been unconscious?" They talked about it for a long time. How difficult is to take care of a child, when they no longer had a true concept of what was "normal" and what was not! Their whole perception of reality had become so skewed….

Following the doctor's instructions, Maggie and Adam kept a close eye on their youngest child. Her recover was miraculously swift. There was no question that the prayers of all the people were answered. Even the doctor, on the follow up visit, was astounded.

It was an eventful summer. Maggie and Adam were excited when his parents invited them up for a boating/fishing trip. The lake was beautiful, and the children had never been fishing from a boat before. It promised to be a wonderful weekend, but this weekend would end in disaster.

Maggie had to admit that she continued to struggle with many of Naomi Joy's behaviors. There were days when she had thoughts and impulses that would shock many of her friends. She knew that she would be unable to endure much longer. There were times, like at the hospital, that she realized what a treasure the child truly was. But most of the time, she found herself exhausted from battling with her.

From morning until night, it was one conflict after another. When she awakened in the morning, Maggie would promise herself that this day would be different. She would be patient and fill each day with activities and distractions that would bring pleasure to them all. Yet, there was always something that seemed to destroy her resolve. Maggie knew that part of it was her own attitude. In spite of her promises, she found it more and more difficult to love this child. Every effort brought further rejection ~ it felt like venom constantly spewed out at her.

The tantrums, screaming, fighting, self-inflicted injuries, hurting the pets…It just never ended and Maggie felt she would never wake up from this nightmare. The frustration took on its own life, turning into anger and resentment. There were times Maggie could no longer bury it and she would lash out verbally, shocking even herself. There were times she thought she could stand it no more. She dreaded to even think about what she could do to Naomi Joy if something didn't change soon.

And it wasn't always at Maggie these behaviors seemed aimed. One day, Maggie had come into the family room where Naomi Joy was playing with her brother's Christmas gift from Mom and Dad—a guinea pig. Maggie saw Naomi

Joy's face, looking down intensely at the little animal in her hands. Her eyes were focused on the small creature, her lips curved in a slight smile.

Maggie looked down at Naomi Joy's hands. They were not gently stroking the helpless guinea pig. They were slowly and carefully squeezing the very life out of it. Maggie rushed over as soon as she realized what was happening. She took the guinea pig, feeling for breath. It was breathing. Barely. Later that day, it died in Jason's hands. Maggie would never forget the look on Jason's face as he looked up, his pet in his hands, and a single tear running down his cheek. Nor would she forget the look on Naomi Joy's face as she squeezed the animal earlier…When confronted with her behavior, Naomi Joy simply shrugged. She said she didn't know why she wanted to hurt the animal. She just wanted to, so she did. It gave her pleasure. Maggie could not understand.

But, today was a new day, a day to enjoy the lake, nature, family…Most of the day, Maggie was able to separate herself from Naomi Joy. Grandma and Grandpa adored her, and enjoyed going out in the boat with her, playing by the shore, gathering pretty stones…Adam also enjoyed her, playing in the sand or splashing in the water.

Jason loved the boat, the lake, and fishing. He even caught a number of fish that made an excellent lunch that afternoon. Grandma let him watch as she cooked them, flattering him about his great talent!

They were all tired when they arrived at Uncle Chad's home that evening. It was way past bedtime and they were tired enough that the children and adults alike were getting out of sorts. All they wanted was to get in bed and settle down for the evening. The Taylors would stay in the camper and the others would all bed down in Uncle Chad's house.

But first, it was time for supper. It was a quick and easy meal, but Naomi Joy decided she didn't want what was offered. She wanted her own dinner, not what everyone else was having. Maggie was growing impatient with her when Grandpa entered the scene.

Grandpa and Grandma did not hesitate in letting Maggie know that she was not the best parent for Naomi Joy. Not that Maggie needed to be told this earth shattering news! This only confirmed Maggie's fears and frustration about her parenting. She knew that Naomi Joy wasn't getting whatever it was she needed. God knows, they had tried, but there seemed to be no answers no matter where they looked. Tonight, she was too tired to be informed of her inadequacy again. When Grandpa let Maggie know that she was being unkind, unfair, and dare we even say, abusive in her insistence that Naomi Joy eat the same supper as everyone else, all the anger, hurt, resentment and frustration seemed to surface in one tremendous explosion.

Maggie was on the way to the bathroom with Naomi Joy when the confrontation reached a head. Maggie picked the child up, walked over to Grandpa, extended her out to him, and shouted, "You know so—much about what she needs—you take her!!!" With that, she allowed Naomi Joy to drop to the floor. Maggie, tears streaming down her face, ran out of the room, leaving the shocked silence behind.

Maggie had a sleepless night. Over and over she replayed the scene in her head. How could she have possibly blown up like that? Why did she create such a confrontation? What in the world was she thinking, using language like that and showing such disrespect for Adam's father? How could she have embarrassed Uncle Chad with her outrageous behavior? She had disgraced herself and her husband. What should she do now? How could she "fix" what she had broken???

Adam talked with her late into the night after the children were bedded down. He tried to reassure her of his love for her, in spite of the crisis. He talked a little bit about the response of the others when Maggie walked out. There had been such anger expressed. His parents had made terrible accusations, and expressed their amazement that Adam allowed this situation to continue. As Maggie wept and sobbed, Adam held her.

Maggie decided to write a note of apology to her father-in-law for reacting to him so negatively and acting in such a dishonorable, disrespectful manner. She wrote one to Uncle Chad for displaying her anger in such a shameful way in his home. When she went to the house, and all were gone, she propped them up on the table, knowing that she had done all she could at this point to rectify a terrible situation.

It was no big surprise to Adam and Maggie that the family disowned them. Such animosity seems to take on a life of its own. It grows and festers like an infected wound. The wound then seeps bitterness to all around. No longer would any of her in laws be in contact with Adam or Maggie or the children, with the sole exception of Kurt and Renee. Kurt and Renee resolved that they would remain neutral. However, it was six years before they were again a part of that extended family. Yet, life continued on and the Taylors had to pick up and move on. This wrenching event must become a part of the past, better filed away and left alone.

It was a lovely spring morning! Maggie looked forward to a quiet Saturday with the children. Adam had to work this morning, but Maggie could take Jason and Naomi Joy to the park. The weather was so unpredictable that they had to enjoy the sunshine on these special spring days! Tomorrow, it might be snowing again! Maggie smiled as she looked out the window. She would get Naomi Joy up and bring their bikes out (Maggie and Jason had been riding them to and from school on nice days). Maggie put Naomi Joy in the little carrier on the back of her bike, and they could have a picnic!

Maggie called Naomi Joy. "Time to comb your hair, Naomi!" There was no response. Oh well, she could go get the little girl. Maggie left the kitchen and went down the stairs to Naomi Joy's room. Naomi was reading, sitting on her bed.

"Time to comb your hair, Honey. We are going to have a picnic at the park today!"

Naomi Joy looked up at her mom. Her almond shaped eyes seemed to be empty, unfocused. "No," said a hollow voice. "Don't do it, don't do it…"

Maggie was shocked. "Naomi, what's wrong?"

"No," repeated the voice, "Don't do it, don't do it…"

It went on like a broken recorder, over and over. Maggie didn't know what to make of it, but she took Naomi Joy's hand and led her up the stairs into the kitchen. "No, don't do it, don't do it. No, don't do it, don't do it. No, don't do it, don't do it…"

While Maggie combed Naomi Joy's hair, putting it into braids, she tried to get Naomi Joy to "come out of it". But Naomi Joy just continued on in that strange hollow voice. When Maggie was finished, Naomi Joy quieted.

"Now, Naomi, what was that about?"

With such calmness, Naomi Joy pointed to a butcher knife in the sink. "You were going to take that knife and cut my head off." There was still no emotion with these horrible words. Maggie was numb with shock. She started remembering other odd things ~~ the bizarre eating patterns, the door being ripped off the hinges, the other voices, as well as this hollow, calm voice, the appliances starting up for no reason, the strange, frightened behavior of the dog. Not long ago Naomi Joy had calmly squeezed a guinea pig to death. And that awful day when someone had slapped her on the back so hard…These things kept happening, and now this. What in the world was going on?

Maggie placed her hand on Naomi Joy's head and began to pray. Maggie did not understand what all of these things meant, but prayer seemed to be the only option now. Naomi Joy jerked away. This, too, was no surprise. Naomi Joy had started acting very angry whenever Maggie and Jason listened to their praise music or the Bible tapes. She didn't ever want to pray...Maggie continued to pray any way. This was **definitely** not behavior that was a product of "a poor marriage relationship"! When Maggie and Adam tried to get counseling for the family, this was always the answer. They were told over and over that they just needed more marriage and/or individual therapy. They loved their pastors, but why couldn't they see this? **Something** spiritual was happening, and it was frightening. And no one seemed willing to help them find answers.

Maggie had been getting prayer at the school, thank God! She and Adam had been in touch with several well-known ministries that they had hoped could help them to understand what was happening and what to do about it. The responses had varied from, "Well, you've lived with it for over four years, a few more days won't matter", to "We just can't take on any long term clients right now...". The frustration was incredible. No one took it seriously, but it sure <u>felt</u> serious to Maggie and Adam! Finally, one of her friends there had introduced Maggie and Adam to her own pastor. They were willing to work with the couple, and the children, but it would take some time. But what about in the mean time? Maggie continued to pray for a few minutes until she felt some strength and comfort come over her. Maybe she had better not mention this to Adam just yet. He was already very shaken by all of the strange things happening in their home.

For the time being, Maggie was able to put the incident out of her mind and enjoy the children, the park, the picnic, and the sunshine.

Later that day, the children were watching a video nearby while Maggie was sitting on the couch in the family room. She glanced up when she heard an unfamiliar sound. What was that? She looked searchingly toward Naomi Joy's bedroom. Yes, there was something...Maggie gasped at what she saw. There was someone moving quietly, slowly into Naomi Joy's bedroom. And what was that in his right hand. A knife, the same knife, upraised as he entered the room.

Maggie blinked and looked again. It was gone. Must be the work of an overactive, slightly stressed mind...But, this time, the uneasiness did not go away...

◆   ◆   ◆

Adam sat bolt upright in the bed, his eyes wide with fear, sweat running down his face. He was breathing heavily. "What should we do? What should we do?" he whispered in a panicked voice.

Maggie sat up, confused. "Adam, what is it? What's wrong?"

Adam was already out of bed. He was searching the room for something, and still muttering under his breath. She heard the words, "It's the kids...it's the kids..." as Adam grabbed the chair from the computer desk and propped it up under the doorknob.

"Adam, don't block the door!" She was alarmed now, too. "If anything happens, I've got to be able to get to the children!"

Adam turned toward her. "No, It *is* the kids! Don't you understand? It *is* the kids!" He was shaking as he got back into the bed. Maggie was totally confused, but she knew there was only one way to make any sense out of the situation. As he lay down, she put her hand on his forehead.

"Father, Adam is so upset, and I don't understand. Please help him to relax and help him to get back to sleep. I pray for Your peace...." Before Maggie was finished praying, Adam was asleep. How odd, thought Maggie, as she too fell asleep.

Maggie watched Adam's face the next morning, wondering what had frightened his so. He was usually the stable one. Well, there was that time Jason cut his eyebrow open when he fell against the piano stool at church and had to have it stitched up. Adam had panicked then. Maggie seldom saw Adam so upset. Adam opened his eyes and smiled at her. "What is it, Love?" he asked.

"I was just thinking about last night. Do you remember anything unusual happening?"

Adam's smile faded. "Yes. I...I'm not sure how to explain it...I saw something...It was so real, not like a dream at all. It was so...so...*real*..."

Adam had Maggie's full attention. Saw something? Her mind went back to yesterday afternoon. She had seen something too, and it, too, had seemed so real...She nodded.

"I saw...Naomi Joy..." He glanced at Maggie. She nodded again, hoping to encourage him to finish.

"I saw Naomi Joy coming into our room. She had her hand up in the air, and there was something in it..."

Maggie swallowed. She had a terrible feeling that she already knew what was in Naomi Joy's hand.

"She was carrying a...a knife...in her upraised hand."

Maggie shook her head. This couldn't be happening! "There is something I have to tell you, Adam. I didn't want to tell you last night, because I knew how hard a time you have had trying to deal with all the...strange things that have been happening lately."

Maggie saw Adam's eyes narrow. She took a deep breath. "Yesterday, when I wanted to comb Naomi's hair…" She told Adam about Naomi's weird response to coming into the kitchen to get her hair combed, and the knife. Then she related what she had seen—and the knife upraised in the man's hand. Slightly different from what Adam had seen, but the similarity was amazing.

Adam and Maggie decided to attend the new church that Maggie's friend had introduced them to. At least they were willing to listen to what was going on without assuming Maggie and Adam had "gone off the deep end"! Adam stated it well, "You can deny you are in a war all you want, but it doesn't keep you from being beat up!" War. A good analogy!

It was later that same afternoon that Martha, an old friend from Maggie's college days, called from Greeley. Any pleasantries were foregone. "Adam, I have been praying, and I know something is wrong down there. I consider myself your mother in the Lord, and of all people you should be sharing with, it should be me. I want to know what is wrong, Adam…"

Adam was taken back. He could not comprehend how it was possible that Martha, so many miles away and to whom they had not spoken for well over a year, knew that something was happening in their lives of this magnitude. He explained, to the best of his ability, the events of the past several years and the frightening things they were seeing now.

Martha was not surprised, and didn't seem to think Maggie and Adam had lost their minds. "We have a prayer/ministry team up here, Adam. We'll put it together and expect to see you next Sunday afternoon. You be praying, too, and we'll see this thing broken!"

Maggie and Adam were not sure what to make of this turn of events, but they DID know they *had* to do something, and soon. Things were getting so far out of control, and there seemed to be no help here. They had never had any education concerning some of these spiritual issues, but there was no doubt now that they were dealing with something outside of their own experience. At this point, Maggie and Adam believed they were dealing with something in addition to the physical. They were even surer of that when they heard, on Saturday, that one of the prayer team had been in a serious car accident, and would not be out of the hospital for some time. Martha assured them that the meeting was still on and she was still expecting them on the following day.

That Sunday morning in May dawned beautiful and clear. Pike's Peak rose in all its majesty, jutting up its white peak into the clear, blue sky. It was a perfect day for a drive up to Greeley! Of course, the fact it was Mothers' Day meant that they would have to stop and have a nice meal on the way. Maggie wasn't sure what this day would hold, but she expected that it would be a Mother's Day she would never forget.

The group consisted of Martha, her husband Bruce and their pastor, Michael. Michael was new to the area, and was bringing revival there. One of the things he seemed to be gifted in was a ministry to families such as the Taylor's ~ families that seemed to have spiritual things going on that they simply could not understand nor battle. Before he was even willing to talk with Naomi Joy, he met with the parents alone.

The pastor told them that regardless of what happened in their prayer time together if they continued to respond in "old ways"; "old behaviors" could be expected to arise once again. When we learn to respond to a child in a certain way, that child will continue in her old patterns as well. They spent time talking and praying. Finally, Michael asked the children to join the adults.

The time of prayer was fairly long, considering the youth of the two children involved. It seemed very intense and very specific. How was it that these people seemed to know things that they could not possibly know? Yet the things they knew were true! They could specify events in Naomi Joy's life that they could not have known. They mentioned specifically the different voices and amazing strength, as well as the high intelligence level.

If the things they stated were true from the Taylor's experience, could it be that those things spoken about Naomi Joy before she had come to America also be true? Surely a tiny baby would not be used in that way. No human being would use an infant sexually! Surely not! Yet, Maggie thought, as one looks back to the flirting, so cute perhaps, but not appropriate in its intensity; back to her physical exploration, and there had been several instances of "playing doctor" that Maggie had tried to push out of her mind. She hadn't even mentioned them to Adam, because she was afraid he would decided she really WAS crazy! She didn't say a word, even though he had been the first to notice Naomi Joy's fascination with things and activity far above her maturity level. That day Adam had wondered what all the noise was in Naomi Joy's room. Naomi Joy was alone, but she was sure making her little crib shake. When he had gone in to check on her, she was obviously receiving great satisfaction from her intimate exploration of her body.

The words "sexual abuse" hung in Maggie's mind once again. But, Naomi Joy had only been six months old when she came to America! If this truly <u>had</u> occurred, if she had truly been "used" sexually in some sort of horrible ceremony…. It HAD to be before she was six months of age! How could *anyone* possibly use a child, a baby, in such a way? Impossible! Surely not! Such things simply do not occur…Yet, those other things…what else COULD it mean? Maggie's mind reeled at the idea. She had spent some time educating herself about the symptoms of sexual abuse victims, but simply could not apply them to this child, to her own daughter!

And the very idea of a *curse*, for heaven's sake! A curse placed on the family to adopt this child? A curse that they would be cursed, just as this "illegitimate" child had placed a curse on her biological, Korean family? Absurd. Impossible. Her mind simply could NOT accept this. Yet…It would explain so much. But, that was speculation on the part of the prayer team. They couldn't know this was true.

Maggie and Adam puzzled over it, watching the pieces slowly fall into place. Yes, it was all starting to make sense now. It would explain so many things. The voices that came out of Naomi Joy that day—that were **not** hers; the strength to rip that door right off the hinges; the piercing hatred Naomi Joy could display; the fits of rage; killing her little pets; her fascination with blood, gore, yet hatred of being dirty herself. There were the physical forms moving in the house, that time "someone" actually struck her; the dog so terrified of an empty room; the appliances switching themselves off and on; pictures jumping off the walls. How about Naomi Joy's absolute intolerance of the Word, the Bible being read, or prayer times? Even her incredible intelligence level.[1]

Toward the end of their prayer time, Jason looked up and glanced at Michael, then to his mother and father. "Strange. I saw a picture…"

Michael smiled gently at the little boy, now six years old. "Yes, son? Can you tell us what you saw?"

Jason spoke with some hesitation as he searched his mind for the right words. "Well," he took a deep breath, "I saw Naomi Joy, down on the floor, on her knees. There was broken glass all around Mommy. She was standing in the middle, looking down at Naomi Joy. Naomi Joy was picking up the glass pieces…." Jason's confusion was obvious, yet the picture seemed so clear in his mind.

Michael nodded. "Yes. That fits in. Here is what I believe it means ~ Naomi Joy will become a healer of broken lives, just as her life has been broken…"

---

1. The purpose of this book is not to delve into the issues of spiritual warfare, etc. However, it must be noted that, in this case, some knowledge of satanic involvement became necessary.

Ever so gently, Michael reached out to Naomi Joy. He tipped her face up, so he could see her beautiful eyes. "Is there something you want to pray about, Naomi Joy?"

Maggie was surprised when Naomi Joy nodded her head. The child reached the point that she left the room when she saw a Bible, heard Scripture read, or a Christian song played. She refused to listen or participate in saying the prayers before meals or bedtime.

Naomi Joy bowed her little head, her braids falling forward. She took her hands out of the bigger hands on each side of hers and folded them. So quietly, but with great emotion, she prayed, "Lord Jesus, please bless my Mommy on this Mother's Day. I really *do* love her. Amen." When Naomi Joy looked up, through her tears, she saw that her mommy, too, was crying.

Maggie was right ~ this was one Mother's Day she would never forget! After the prayer time, there was a little celebration with the family. Martha had prepared a special dessert, and all joined in the fun. Naomi Joy sat on her mother's lap, and the two of them shared a very special day together.

It was the following Sunday, in their new church, that the oddest thing happened. There was a visitor sitting behind the Taylor family. As the service came to an end, the gentleman tapped Adam on the shoulder. "I feel I have a word for you about your daughter..."

Adam smiled down at Naomi Joy and then at the stranger. "Yes?"

"This probably sounds funny. I don't even know you! But I feel like I am supposed to tell you that this child will grow up and become a healer of broken lives. I don't know exactly what that means, but maybe you do."

Adam swallowed hard. "Yes," he whispered, "I believe I might...Thank you."

It was about two weeks later that this same message was repeated, another stranger, another church service, but the same word.

Maggie remembered a Scripture ~ by the word of two or three witnesses. Something like that. She hid these words in her heart, to recall them on many an occasion when discouragement threatened to overcome hope. *"A healer of broken lives..."*

There was something that Maggie and Adam could not understand, even with the teaching they were receiving. They were often afraid to say anything anyway ~ it seemed like some of these things that happened around Naomi Joy were so strange that people did not believe the stories. There see to be situations in which it is best to ponder them and not ask questions. Maggie remembered when Mary, the mother of Jesus, "pondered these things in her heart". Maggie was nothing like that godly woman, but she would just ponder these things and only discuss them with Adam.

When they had arrived home after their prayer time with the little group in Greeley, Naomi Joy seemed to have...forgotten...things. Simple things. She couldn't remember the lay out of the house and was genuinely confused when it came to finding her own bedroom and the upstairs bathroom. She could no longer tie her shoes, and would cry in her frustration. And the amazing skill she had shown in her reading was gone. She had to learn to read all over again.

How could this be? Maggie and Adam discussed it at length. There was a definite change in Naomi Joy. Along with the loss of certain skills, she also showed a greater responsiveness to Maggie, and no longer resisted going to church, Sunday School, listening to Bible stories...Even her face displayed a change. Her expression was softer, calmer, and more serene. They couldn't clearly define what had happened, but a new peace descended upon the home and its occupants. Even "outsiders" seemed to notice a difference, and would comment on it. Maggie looked at her two lovely children, her faithful husband, the wonderful job ~ and was content.

Christmas arrived at last! What a joyous time of year! Nothing could dampen the children's enthusiasm. And who could be around two happy little ones, and not feel that same sense of anticipation? As the big day drew nearer, the excitement grew. The tree was up and beautifully trimmed. Anyway, the children thought it was beautiful! After all, they had decorated it themselves! Christmas things could be seen all over the house, proclaiming the birth of the Lord. All was provided for the traditional turkey dinner. How they all looked forward to it!

Daddy seemed a bit late returning from his little shopping excursion. Jason and Naomi Joy played on the floor near the front door while Mommy relaxed and read nearby. The Christmas music softly played in the background and the feeling of peace permeated the whole house.

Finally, they heard the car pull up! Jason raced to the door. Since he arrived there first, he got to open the door and welcome Daddy in from the cold! Naomi Joy and Jason were clapping with excitement. "Daddy's home! Daddy's home!"

Daddy spent several minutes with the little ones before asking Maggie to join him in the kitchen. He wanted to talk to her alone.

"Maggie, thank you for not opening the door any earlier. I was worried that they would come in and really disrupt the household. I told them they couldn't come in, if they couldn't treat you and me with a level of respect in front of the children."

Maggie stared at her husband in absolute confusion. "What are you talking about? Jason opened the door as soon as you pulled into the driveway."

Adam shook his head. "I have been home for, probably, 30–45 minutes."

With a laugh, Maggie dismissed the joke. "Adam, you are such a tease!"

Gently Adam placed his hands on Maggie's shoulders. "No, Maggie, I have been home for some time now. I was out in the driveway, trying to talk with my mom and father. Couldn't you hear him shouting at me? He was standing right on the doorstep, shouting that he would see his grandchildren."

Maggie could see that Adam was serious. But how could that be? They had heard nothing, except the car pulling up, the slam of the car door, and then Adam's entrance into the house. There had been no shouting, no time elapsed at all!

It was not until Adam took his wife into the garage and showed her the packages that Grandpa had thrown into the snow bank on his angry departure, that she would believe him. How could this be explained? Outside their door, an argument had ensued over a half-hour period of time. Yet, inside that same door, peace had reigned, and it seemed that no time had passed at all! Adam and Maggie knew this could not be; yet, somehow, it was true. Could this be another miracle?

PART III

School Days ~ Kindergarten

Naomi Joy was excited to join Jason and her mommy on their way to school. It was a great event, going to "big kid" school! No more preschool or day-care now! When mommy went to school, she would go to school. She was absolutely thrilled, and the excitement shone from out of her big, dark brown eyes! Her hair was braided and held in it beautiful barrettes and bows. Her first day of school dress, finished weeks ahead of time, made her look like a princess—anyway, that is what her daddy and mommy told her! She had her brand new backpack, filled with all kinds of new school goodies, pencils, crayons, paper…She chatted happily with Jason all the way to school.

Naomi Joy loved school She was obviously a gifted student, far above her peers academically. Even her handwriting was a work of art! But she seemed unable, as the days and weeks passed, to relate to her classmates in appropriate ways. Her relationships were strained when, at one moment, she could be utterly charming, and the next, mean and hurtful. She was finding new a creative ways to get her own way ~ surprising even the most clever of her unsuspecting peers. Many times, Maggie saw a repetition of the funny episode of the "Cup Switch" Naomi Joy had perpetrated on her older brother a couple of years before, only they weren't so funny now…. The victim would be baffled, and unsure as to how to respond.

She was, however, a delight in the classroom, quickly grasping concepts and maintaining a high standard academically. She was reading several grades above her level the very day she started in kindergarten. Her giftedness showed in every area—math, reading, handwriting, science, and health—everywhere with the exception of P.E. Often, she was "too ill" to attend class, and when she did, she often sat out. Her gross motor skills were far behind her other skills. Running, kicking, riding a two wheeler, skipping ~ all of these skills took a great deal of work to develop, and Naomi Joy was behind her peers in every one of them. This made it very difficult, for in no other area did she have to experience the "failure" of not being first, the best, the top of the class. No amount of consolation or encouragement seemed to help her reach a more accepting attitude.

Maggie found that her little kindergarten students loved having "homework" ~ just like the older children!! So, whenever she ran off paperwork or had extra copies of any handouts, she would run off extras to place in the "Homework" box. The children could select one or two papers each afternoon and return the finished product the next day. Naomi Joy loved the extra work as well.

One afternoon, she spent her time meticulously coloring and completing a page of homework. Maggie stood nearby, washing dishes. She turned when Naomi Joy held up her paper and asked in utmost seriousness, "Mommy, do you think Mrs. Taylor will like my work?"

Maggie laughed in delight. Naomi Joy had been instructed to call her mother "Mrs. Taylor" at school, just as the other children did. "Yes, darling, I happen to know that Mrs. Taylor will absolutely LOVE your work!" She embraced the child as Naomi Joy smiled.

As the year moved on, Maggie noticed more and more of the "old" behaviors returning. Naomi Joy still had a wet bed almost every morning, but that wasn't a big problem. Except when Naomi Joy had a guest over and would invite them into her room. Then she would say, in a most deriding voice, "My mom REFUSES to wash my things. Isn't this just gross?" Then would follow tales of the other, awful things to which mother subjected the innocent child…

Maggie wasn't sure how to handle this, but she rarely allowed Naomi Joy to invite friends over. It seemed like Naomi Joy had so many grievances to share with her little friends, but arguing and pointing out the facts had little impact on the child's imagination.

The lies continued to grow. The difficult thing was that often Naomi Joy would build a story on just enough fact that it appeared she had "evidence" that the story was true! They were usually believable. If not because they were based on a shred of truth, then because they were so intricate that one knew they simply must be true; no child could make up such a detailed story!

Even at home, Naomi Joy created amazing stories with great attention to detail. She described one such episode including details on what clothes she was wearing and what she was eating at the time. Because of that story, a family joke became, "…and remember? I was eating cucumbers at the time…".

After a time, as kindergarten passed, and Naomi Joy moved on out of Maggie's class, and her stories became more believable, there were times Maggie questioned her own sanity. Maybe this or that story was true. Perhaps Maggie just had forgotten it, or seen the events in a distorted manner. Maybe she really DID sign that permission slip, that schoolwork paper with the dark, red "F" on it, and just couldn't remember it. Surely, Naomi Joy couldn't forge her handwriting THAT well...Perhaps Naomi Joy had asked permission to go to that event, and Maggie granted it, but was simply too distracted to remember...Maybe these accusing fingers pointed her way were right...perhaps she was a poor mother, showing obvious favoritism toward Jason and leaving Naomi Joy out more and more...Perhaps....

In kindergarten, all the students took breaks together, to help maintain order. They went to recess, had snack, sang together. They went to the bathroom to wash up and attend to any other business, as a group. This wasn't true as Naomi Joy moved into first and second grade.

The bathroom was at the end of the hall. The hall walls on one side were lined with coat hooks where all the children hung their coats—and their lunch boxes. Hot lunches were not served at the school, so each child brought his own meal and stowed it under his coat. Mysteriously, food consistently disappeared out of those boxes. Often, a child would open up his box to find it totally empty. It was really bad when large numbers of children would have no lunch left at lunch-time—all on the same day. There were occasions when there was no one left with a lunch to share, except for a few carrot sticks or a stray radish or two. No one, except Naomi Joy, who was happy to share a bit here, a bit there...

As time went on, it wasn't just food that disappeared, but jewelry, money, make up, expensive pens, finger nail polish...It was very irritating the day the frosting vanished off the birthday cake set aside for the after school celebration of another teacher's birthday. Often teachers' things would simply disappear right out of their desk drawers. Nothing was safe, not stickers, personal items, science equipment, and, of course, money. Sometimes fairly large sums of money would seem to evaporate into thin air; the children's' collected milk money, for instance.

Fund raising projects were a nightmare. Either the candy or the money would be gone, leaving without a trace. Many, many times Adam and Maggie had to shell out money to cover various "unexpected expenses", because they KNEW but could not prove, what was happening. Those that believed that Naomi Joy was behind these things, blamed Adam, and more particularly, Maggie for their poor parenting, lack of leadership, being too strict, or not strict enough. The accusations were many.

Maggie tried everything she could think of. No amount of "natural conse-quences", time out, recompense, talking, discussion, pleading, or even spanking, had any effect at all. Except to confirm Naomi Joy's image as a poor, mistreated, little thing.

On one occasion, after having been caught stealing, Maggie informed Naomi Joy that she would need to stay in the kindergarten room for recess. As she left the room, Maggie thought of the kindergarten snack in the closet. She knew Naomi Joy also knew where they were. Maggie had a meeting and had to get there; she was already late.

"Naomi Joy," she said, "stay OUT of the closet. You are not to be taking things out of there—you need to just sit there and finish that work…" With that, Maggie hurried out the door.

When Maggie arrived back at her room a short time later, she saw Naomi Joy suddenly sit down at the table where Maggie had last seen her. She knew immediately. "Naomi Joy, what have you been doing? Is your work finished?"

Naomi Joy nodded her head.

"And what is in your mouth?"

"Nothing…" responded her daughter.

"Stand up, please." Sure enough, there were a half dozen graham crackers on the bench, a little worse for wear after having a young lady sitting on them. Maggie was furious, both with herself for having been so careless, and Naomi Joy for taking the snack. Her voice came out several octaves higher than usual. "You are in here for stealing, and you turn around and steal from me????" Maggie could feel the adrenaline rising. She also knew that if she didn't force herself to stop now, she would lose control. She didn't dare unleash her temper, not here, not now…Her hands were balled up into fists, her knuckles white with anger. She gritted her teeth, feeling wave after wave of white rage, threatening to sweep her up in the flood. "Get out of here right now." she choked out, "we'll deal with this later."

As Naomi Joy left, Maggie thought she saw the shadow of a smile on her face. Maggie sat down heavily and tried to regain some composure before the afternoon kindergarten class was due. It infuriated her when these things happened—and that smile that Naomi Joy wore when she knew she had the upper hand once again, only intensified the fury. Maggie had never considered herself a rageful person, but these last few years changed that. Naomi Joy seemed to take great delight in pushing her mother right up against the wall. She seemed to take pleasure in watching her mother lose all control. Maggie was concerned that, one day, she would lose any restraint she had left, and who knew what would happen then?

Things seemed to go better for awhile, after that visit up in Greeley. But it hadn't lasted long. Maybe it was worse now than it had been before. Maggie shook her head. Naomi Joy. How could she have so misnamed a child? What was left now? And how would she ever survive this child??? She didn't hold out much hope.

1st Grade ~ The Elf

The snow continued to fall steadily. The cold could rip right through a person. Maggie went down the stairs where the elementary age children were playing, waiting for the whistle, letting the children know it was time to line up and be ready for classes to begin. She laughed a little as she saw the huge pile of coats, hats, gloves, boots…How these children ever managed to match their boots and gloves back up she would never know. No wonder the Lost and Found box was overflowing.

The supervising parents were busy with clusters of children. The noise was absolutely deafening. Mercy! She glanced around to see if she could see Jason and Naomi. There was Jason, involved in a challenging game of marbles. And Naomi was…ahhh, right there, beside the lunch boxes. Why was she not surprised???!!! Of course, where else would she be? All this noise and confusion was a good cover for her "grazing". No matter that she had eaten a huge breakfast and had her own lunch. There was always room for more!

Maggie wandered slowly over to her daughter. "Naomi."

Naomi's head jerked up and she looked innocently at her mother. She smiled her beautiful smile. "Hi, Mom. Is it time to line up?"

"Before we line up, Naomi, I need to check your pockets. Naomi looked about herself, looking as innocent as the day is long. "Why?'

Mom smiled grimly. "You know why, Naomi."

Naomi was becoming angry now. "Why? You have no proof of anything! You have no reason at all to check my pockets!"

"Please come here, Naomi. There is no need for a scene." Maggie placed her hand in Naomi's pocket, first one and then the other. How could this much stuff fit in those little pockets? Two candy bars, a granola bar, three sticks of gum, and a nickel. Maggie held out her open hands and showed Naomi what she had found. "Now, how do you suppose these got in your pockets?"

Naomi didn't miss a beat. With a straight face, she answered, "The elf put them there."

Maggie was stunned. That was a new one. She looked from the stuff in her hands to Naomi. She couldn't help it. A laugh started low in her chest and just rose up until it poured out of her mouth. She laughed so hard tears began to run down her cheeks. Other students were looking at this strange spectacle. They thought Mrs. Taylor was a bit crazy, they loved it! But what could be so funny?

Naomi looked at her mother with righteous anger. "See," she yelled, "even when I tell the truth, you won't believe me! It *was* the elf! I tell you the truth, and you laugh!" She seemed genuinely enraged and stood with her hands in tight little fists.

Maggie fought for control. It was just too funny! She tried to talk through her chuckles. "Really, Naomi, an *elf*? Now what would you say if your little girl told you an *elf* snuck stuff into her pockets?" The last part came out choked with a laugh! "An *elf*, Naomi?! Surely you can do better than that!"

Naomi stared hard at her mother. She didn't seem to notice the other children gathering around. Her hands were still tightly clenched. "You think I stole it, don't you?! Well, you are WRONG! The elf took it and put it in my pockets, and that's the truth!" Angrily she stalked away, leaving Maggie holding the stolen goodies, staring after her daughter in disbelief. The other students looked from daughter to mother and back to Naomi again. "An elf ~ she said an elf took it. Well," another laugh escaped, "let's see if we can get this stuff back where it belongs. Please check your lunch boxes and let's see where this goes…" She laughed again, "An elf yet!" she muttered.

This was not to be the end of the "Elf Episode". Many times the elf returned, placing things in the most unusual places. There was the time Maggie and Naomi were working together to clean the little girl's room. Naomi loved the hearts her mother and stenciled around the room, and the pretty heart canopy over her bed. She had a dust ruffle that matched, and even the cushion on the chair at her vanity was of the same pattern. Maggie pulled the dresser away from the wall so they could clean up the papers that had slid behind it. "What the….?" Maggie looked more closely at the back of the dresser. What were those little globs all over the back? At least they smelled decent, like…peppermint.

"Naomi, there are wads of gum all over the back of your dresser. Why would that be?" Would Maggie ever learn to state facts without asking stupid questions that just gave Naomi an opportunity to be creative?

"Oh," Naomi said nonchalantly, "the elf put them there…"

Maggie could not believe that "the elf" had been so busy with her own gum! "Naomi, I am sick and tired of hearing about this elf!" Her voice was rising. "You went in my room, stole more of my gum and saved it all on the back of your dresser! What in God's name are you saving it for???!!!"

Naomi was the epitome of calm. "I didn't take it. The elf got it from somewhere and gave it to me. I chewed it all and saved it back there for later."

Maggie felt like slapping that lying mouth. Or worse. "Naomi, you tell me the truth and you tell me now! You stole that gum out of my room!"

"No!", yelled Naomi back, "I told you the elf took it and that is the truth!"

Maggie was so angry at being violated **again** that she knew she would do something stupid. "Young lady," she said through gritted teeth, "you scrape every piece of MY gum off YOUR dresser, and have it in the trash before I come back down to this room, or I'll..."

The defiance in Naomi's face was unbelievable. "You'll *what*, Mother? I can't help it what the elf does! *What* will you do?!"

Maggie's voice was far too loud when she responded, "JUST DO IT!!!" She stormed off in a rage. Behind her, she heard, as she slammed the door, "Huh! The elf did it!"

Maggie's anger increased. She'd love to rip that lying tongue right out of her mouth! Naomi *always* had to have the last word! She constantly violated Maggie's things! If it wasn't food, it was jewelry. If it wasn't jewelry, it was make up. There was always something. Where would this all end? One of them was going to end up dead! Either she would wring that child's neck, or shoot herself!

Maggie charged out the door. She ran as fast as her anger could push her. This anger ~ what could she do with it? *Nothing* ever changed. Naomi stole and lied and screamed and...Maggie's feet pounded the pavement. Every step was like a punch into this nameless, black anger. No matter what she did, *nothing* would change. She was being swallowed up in her anger, resentment, and bitterness and there was absolutely no help. No one had answers. There would be no end to the nightmare! Harder and harder she ran. No answers! The rest of her life in this nightmare! It would never end! No one really understood! Everyone saw the charming, sweet, pretty, polite little girl. What was this evil that Maggie saw every moment of her day? Why, why had this happened? Maggie's heart felt like it would beat itself right out of her chest. Her breathing was ragged and painful. She had run as far as she could. But the anger was still there, burning, burning, burning. She was too tired to hit Naomi now, too tired to yell or scream. All that was left were tears, more tears. And the burning...Maggie sat on the grass with her head in her hands. She had to go back, pretend she was okay, cook dinner for Adam, and smile sweetly at him. Let the tears flow, but they would never quench this burning. How much longer before she would blow? How much longer before there would be nothing left? How much longer could she hold on to her sanity? Burning...burning...burning...

It was worse now that Naomi was no longer in Maggie's class. As she had moved on to first grade, the behaviors worsened, simply because the teacher could not keep a vigilant eye on Naomi and be effective with the other children as well. Maggie liked the new first grade teacher. She had a daughter much like Naomi. Often, over lunch, she and Rebecca would talk and share their experiences. Rebecca's daughter was also adopted; in fact, Rebecca shared with Maggie how they had gotten Mary through the social services organization there in town. Every now and then, as she listened and thought, Maggie wondered if she shouldn't consider approaching Adam about adopting again. It was possible that they would have another wonderful experience like they had with Jason. God knew she could sure use one! But, no...

Mary behaved in many of the same ways Naomi did—they seemed to be a matched pair. They both could not leave food alone; they both were experts at manipulation and lying. They both could steal just about anything from anyone. Often Rebecca echoed Maggie's emotions and the roller coaster ride those emotions seemed to be. Sometimes Rebecca could offer a word of encouragement, or Maggie one to Rebecca. They could relate to one another in a way Maggie had not experienced before. And, Rebecca could make Maggie find humor in the situation. Often they laughed at the absurdity of their common situation. None-the-less, the stress was once again taking its toll on Maggie—as well as the rest of the family.

It wasn't long after this, that Mr. Roderro, the principal of the school, came to Maggie. "Maggie, I know that something is wrong. You don't bring your problems to work with you, and don't generally talk about them. But I can tell that you are hurting, and I want to be able to help."

His sensitivity and compassion touched Maggie. She shared some of the story with him. He had prayed with the staff—in fact, they met once a week for devotions and prayer. Therefore, he was aware of some of the stresses in the lives of each of the staff members, but Maggie had never shared as deeply as she did now. She even shared her fear that she might not be able to continue on much longer this way.

Mr. Roderro was sympathetic and understanding. He had already finished raising his own children, and had a good idea of what was "normal" and what was not. He had also watched Naomi (and Mary!) and knew full well that there were some "special needs" here. He respected and admired Maggie, and wanted to see no further pain come into her life. And he could help.

"Perhaps" he suggested, "you need a break, Maggie. You need time away from the situation so that you can regain some perspective. I know of some people that might be willing to have Naomi come into their home for a time. She could still come to school and be involved in the activities here. Would you like me to check out the possibility?"

Maggie nodded and tried to smile. She knew he was right. She was losing any perspective she ever had. She would talk to Adam about it and see what he thought of the idea.

Adam was in agreement. Not only did Maggie need a break, even he did! He was struggling more and more with the odd behaviors of his little princess, and was increasingly concerned as Naomi grew. The problems were intensifying, and the need for a break was great.

So it was that Naomi went to stay with the youth pastor from the church in which the school met, along with his wife. Naomi could still come to school since they lived just blocks away. She could stay for two weeks, which would give Naomi, Adam and Jason the break they needed. This young couple was also interested in working with children with Attachment Disorder, and this would give them an opportunity to see if this was something that was truly possible for them. Perhaps they could be more objective and encourage the whole Taylor family in some way. It was worth a try!

Maggie and Adam kept in contact with the pastor and his sweet wife as regularly as possible, giving suggestions and receiving updates and insights the couple had about Naomi.

During this time, Naomi reverted to wetting the bed again, and was even wetting during the day, but only in reaction to certain things. Her caretakers wanted to "bless" Naomi, so did a few special things with and for her. Each time Naomi received from them, she would wet herself! This wasn't all that uncommon—when Naomi did well she usually had to sabotage herself in some way. It seemed almost as if she couldn't handle praise or the threat of closeness with any caretaker. Why couldn't she allow herself to succeed? Why couldn't she allow herself to be happy? Or loved? It was a time of many questions—but as always—few answers.

2nd Grade—Farewell to the Elf!

Naomi had taken up piano this year. She seemed to have a natural gift for music, even from the beginning. She had her teacher buffaloed for awhile. Naomi could hear a piece played once, and go home and play it by ear. The teacher didn't realize that Naomi couldn't read a note of music for quite some time. Naomi would ask the teacher to play each piece. Some how she retained the piece, would go home and play it on the piano! She was very unhappy when the teacher realized what was happening and told Naomi to go home, try it by the music in the book and come back to following week to see where she needed practice. It made all the difference ~ suddenly Naomi had to work at her music.

Naomi had so much trouble staying committed to any project that she was not able to quickly master. Her perfectionism complicated matters ~ if she couldn't master a task quickly and perfectly, she would draw away and avoid it. This characteristic seemed to be compensated by other skills ~ such as this amazing ability to play by ear.

One night, as she worked at her latest piece, Adam sat in his rocking chair listening. Suddenly, the music stopped, and he heard quick steps coming up the stairs.

Naomi's eyes were wide with fear. "Daddy, I saw something! I saw something!"

Adam looked at his daughter, beautiful even with the fear on her face. "Saw what, Princess?"

"I saw—I was practicing and—it was in Jason's room!"

"Take a deep breath, Naomi. Then try to tell me what you saw in Jason's room."

Naomi took a deep breath and tried to explain. "Well, I was practicing and I looked over at Jason's room because the light came on. Then I saw someone walk across the room, and then the light turned off! Daddy, no one was even in the room! Jason is out with Mom and his light was off and...and..."

Adam didn't miss a beat. "Well, Naomi, you are the one who invited "the elf" in. Why are you so frightened at seeing him tonight?"

Naomi looked at her father's face. He seemed serious. She turned. "I think I'd better go finish practicing."

Adam pondered the whole scene. Where in the world did that answer come from? Why in the world did he say that? Frowning, he returned to his paper. And Naomi never spoke of her elf again…

It wasn't long after that, however, that Naomi had a frightening dream. She rarely spoke of her dreams—not surprisingly! Maggie wondered if she ever slept long enough to have dreams! Naomi came to her daddy, seeking his comfort.

"Daddy, I dreamed that you, and mommy, took me to a strange building. It was a big building. You both got out of the car, and walked me to the building. But," Naomi shuddered at the memory. It was so real to her, even now. "but, when it was time to go, I didn't get in the car with you."

Adam looked into his daughter's beautiful, dark eyes. "Yes, honey? You didn't get in the car? Why?"

"I don't know, Daddy. But you got in and Mommy got in. I stayed there, standing at the door. You drove away, and when I looked in the window, Mommy was crying. I think you were too. You both waved at me, and I called you. You wouldn't come back, and I felt all alone. I knew I couldn't go home with you. I was scared, Daddy!"

Rarely had Adam seen such vulnerability in his daughter. He held her tightly, smoothing her hair. He wasn't sure what to say. Finally he said, "Honey, sometimes you make choices that hurt you and hurt us." How to put this into words…"Sometimes, a child has to go somewhere to get help, to get better. And I hope that doesn't happen to you." Not very comforting, but it was on his heart and came out his mouth. "I want to always protect you, but there are choices that are made sometimes, that even I can't protect you from. But, I will always try, Naomi. I will always try…"

Holding Naomi, Adam sighed deeply. He would think back to that day often. It was a difficult decision, but the time had come for Maggie to say good-bye once again to teaching. She dearly loved her job, and the people with whom she worked. However, too many changes were taking place, which she could not condone. The members of the school board were at odds with one another. It looked as if Mr. Roderro was going to retire. This was difficult for Maggie—he had been there for her on several occasions when she was at the end of her rope. He had always shown her respect as a professional, friend and woman. He never failed to be gentle with her, unlike many of her other "friends". In additions, school discipline diminished every day, making it more and more difficult to deal with situations needing more attention than the average. Maggie and Adam talked at great length about the decision and decided that it was time to slow down again, regain some perspective, work directly with Jason and Naomi, and begin to support the school that met at their own church.

Adam went to the board meeting with Maggie that evening. Maggie had written a formal letter of resignation, clearly stating the reasons for leaving. She read it out loud and gave each board member a copy. Adam sat next to her, his arm protectively around her shoulder.

Her voice started out slowly as she read, but strong. As she progressed through the letter, the tears began and reading was difficult. Maggie hated crying, and rarely did in public. She tried to stop—it was so hard to get the words out. Yet, she read on, until she had read the whole letter.

There was silence for several minutes when she finished. Adam squeezed her shoulder and she smiled gratefully at him through her tears. The group appeared stunned. Soon enough, the talk began. Maggie would not be swayed from her decision. It was a shame to quit now—the school needed students. Many of the parents would withdraw their children when they found out this kindergarten teacher was leaving. There would be questions they didn't care to answer. Yet, Maggie and Adam stood firm.

Indeed, enrollment did drop, even as Maggie talked with parents and encouraged them to keep their children in the school. She felt badly, but knew that, with time, they would forget Maggie Taylor, and the new teacher would be as much loved by the parents, teachers and children as she had been. Time has a way of doing that…She would miss it too, but she knew there were other things in store for her…And life is filled with good-byes.…

PART IV

Changes

The new school seemed like a good change for Naomi, Jason and Maggie. Naomi had many friends because of their membership in the church, as did Jason. Maggie could volunteer and be involved with the children, but also had free time to pursue some other interests. The adjustment was a little difficult. Rather than the contained classroom situation they were accustomed to, in this school each student had their own station where they could work. The idea was that this would cut down on distractions and each child could work at his own pace. For some children, like Naomi who were self-starters and well motivated, this plan seemed to work well. For other children, like Jason, who didn't particularly enjoy the school environment any way and had little interest in book learning, it was not nearly as successful. Jason continued to struggle here, as he had in the previous school. His struggle distressed his mother, and she helped as she could…

Naomi, too, struggled. Here it was also difficult for her to maintain friendships. These friends were unique in that they were the same children with whom her family socialized, went to church, and now, even went to school! They had enough contact with her to know that Naomi's view of what a friendship is and their own view was vastly different. In spite of this, however, there were those friends that gathered around Naomi because of her charisma, because they might be able to "help" her, or because their personality blended well with hers.

Maggie worked one or two days a week, as an aid with the youngest children. It was helpful because it meant that she could be available for the next crisis, and it was an excellent way for her keep tabs on what was going on within the school.

It did seem like things were calming down again. Jason was working hard, but could move at a pace more comfortable for him. Naomi was learning to fit into the structure of the school system ~ and her "acting out" occurred more in that environment than at home. Adam seemed to be enjoying his job, and Maggie felt somewhat content.

Maggie and Adam continued to monitor Naomi's progress, and both wondered if it would be possible to add a child to their family. They had learned a great deal about Attachment Disorder ~ maybe they could help other children.

They began to check into some options. There was a foster/adopt program with the Department of Social Services. As they examined this possibility, it began to be an exciting adventure that infected the whole household. Naomi and Jason were so excited about the thought of a new child coming into their lives. Maggie and Adam loved babies, and the thought of another one was like a breath of fresh air. The idea of the child being a foster child first of all, was a good one ~ it would allow a "trial period" to evaluate the whole situation. Perhaps they could venture out just a little bit, pray a lot, and see what happened.

Fall came and went. Winter was beginning to mellow out, still cool, and still a possibility of snow any time. After all, March tended to be one of the heaviest snow fall months in this part of the world! And it was Adam's birthday ~ March 13th. Maggie and the children were at school.

Maggie, Jason, and Naomi had talked about how they could make this day special, but they had not counted on just how special it would be.

The principal of the school came to get Maggie. There was a telephone call from the "birthday boy"!

"Hi, Maggie! How would you feel about not one, but two children?"

Maggie was taken aback. "Excuse me? What are you talking about?"

Adam could barely contain his excitement. "The caseworker just called. She has two children she needs a place for."

Maggie thought a moment, her excitement rising too. "Well...Tell me about them..."

The two children were biracial. The little boy was four years old and his sister, three. When Maggie asked when they could see them, Adam gave her the really big surprise. "In about forty five minutes! She needs to know our answer right away!"

Maggie laughed. "Sure, why not? Happy birthday, Daddy!!!"

The timing couldn't have been better. School was just dismissed. Maggie caught Naomi on her way out of the classroom. "Naomi!"

Naomi swung around at the sound of her mother's voice. "How would you feel about a little brother?"

Naomi's eyes lit up! She loved little ones and had talked of nothing else for months. She had plans already of where the baby would sleep, what they would play, where they would go..."A brother?!"

"And a sister!"

Naomi ran to Maggie. "Two? We get two???!" Maggie's excitement was clearly reflected in Naomi's face. "How old?"

Maggie told Naomi the few details she had and told her that they had to get ready very quickly. For heaven's sake, they didn't even have two beds!

Naomi ran down the stairs to find Jason, telling everyone she met (the entire school!) the exciting news. Jason could hardly believe it either. They both met Maggie at the car, full of questions, for which Maggie had absolutely no answers.

When the trio reached home, Maggie called the church prayer chain with the news. It spread quickly through the church and soon people were arriving with gifts for the two children. Before little Troy and Tammi even arrived, they had new clothes, toys, bedding...As the caseworker arrived with the children, even the second bed showed up in a friend's car!

The children and Maggie were watching out the window when the caseworker's car pulled up. She unloaded two little ones. "Oh, Adam, they are so cute! Come and see them! They are SO cute!!!" All three were dancing in their excitement. Adam came to join them, adding a little calm to the chaos.

"Well, let's go meet them. But calm down first ~ we don't want to scare the little tikes. They look frightened enough already!"

Troy and Tammi were indeed adorable. They came to the Taylors with the clothes on their backs and no more. Through the generosity of the church, that problem was quickly remedied.

Adam went to Kentucky Fried Chicken and brought home a bucket of chicken and all the 'fixins" to go with it. All four children were excited! Adam asked a blessing over the family, all six of them!

Troy acted as if he had never eaten at a table before! He inhaled his dinner. When it came time for food to be eaten with a fork, he never picked his up. He simply lowered his chin to the table, tipped the plate and scraped the food in. It was a good thing that the Taylors had taken the classes required of foster/adoptive parents and had learned that nothing should surprise them! So, this would be one of the first things they would work on—table manners!

That night, Maggie tucked the children in to their little beds. She showed them how they could pray before bed to someone in Heaven named "Jesus". As she tucked Troy into bed, he looked at her with those big, brown eyes. "Will we get to eat tomorrow, too?"

Maggie was a bit taken back by the question, but answered evenly, "Of course, Troy! In fact, at *this* house we eat THREE times—we call the first meal breakfast."

"Well, what do you eat for breakfast?"

Maggie thought for a minute. "Well, I think we will have pancakes..."

A smile crossed Maggie's lips as Troy licked his own. "...and we'll have an egg,"

Troy's eyes were gleaming.

"...some apple slices, and orange juice."

A smile of contentment crossed the little boy's face.

It became a part of the nighttime ritual. Each night, Troy would ask what would be for breakfast; Maggie would tell him, and he would cuddle down into his blankets with a smile. Before long, Troy and Tammi learned the names of each meal, and the names of different foods served at those meals. They were most familiar with hamburgers, pizza and tacos. Anything else was labeled "meat", or "fruit" and the two children seemed unaware of names for specific items. Could there be a connection between the names of those three items, and the fact that the home in which they had lived was located in an apartment building just behind fast food restaurants that served them?

It wasn't until much later that Maggie and Adam picked up on statements Troy would make about his life "before". These statements often put pieces of the puzzle of the children's' broken lives together. Troy knew a great deal about dumpsters found behind such businesses...

It was a telling remark when Jason came up from his room one afternoon and remarked, "You know, Mom, I've been thinking. Troy was just telling me that he had a whole bunch of Legos at his house—but he didn't get to bring them with him. I sure have a lot of stuff, and he has nothing..."

It was then that Maggie knew helping foster children was going to be good for her own children. Jason and Naomi quit always looking to themselves and started truly caring about some one else, and hurting for their pain. Naomi loved playing with little "TammiBug's" hair, helping her try on different little outfits, and thinking of games to play. Jason took to calling Troy "My Man", which tickled the little boy to death.

One day, after the foster children had been with them for about six months, Maggie had Troy and TammiBug on the playground, and a black gentleman noticed Troy. He called Troy "brother", to which Troy puffed out his chest and stoutly replied, "My big brother calls me MY MAN!" Well, what can one say to such a response?!

Maggie and Adam could not believe the changes in their children. They could not understand where such nurturing had sprung from in Naomi. She was astounding in her gentleness and love for these little ones. Maggie reflected on the past nine years. Naomi's life had not been one of nurturing or even receiving nurturing. Where in the world did she learn this??? Perhaps something had happened in Naomi. Could it be possible that the tears Maggie had shed for this child meant something after all? And Jason! What a great big brother! He loved rough housing with Troy. And it was entirely mutual!

Maggie had never seen a child such as Troy. While the Taylor family had NEVER laughed so much at the absolutely delightful things these very deprived children said and did, they also feared for Troy's safety. The first time they realized it, was the day Troy tried taking his new skateboard to the top of the slide outside. Adam did not wait to see if Troy would actually try to skateboard down the slide. He rushed out, grabbed the little boy off the slide and started to teach him the proper use of a skateboard! Fortunately, Jason enjoyed his own skate board and was willing to work with Troy until they could go out together for fun, and not bodily damage!

There was also the time that Troy decided to see what would happen if he ran his finger down the edge of the full-length mirror, just to see what would happen. As the blood gushed out of the cut (that required numerous stitches in the emergency room), he simply stared, amazed at the effect. He didn't shed a tear, even as the doctor stitched it up. Funny thing, though. The very first thing he did when he got the stitches out was try that edge again. Because Adam had wrapped all the edges with tape, it didn't cut his finger open. "Look, Daddy, it didn't cut it!" he exclaimed in wonder!

Troy decided that it was time to learn to ride a "two wheeler". Maggie and Adam found a small, sturdy bike at a garage sale and had picked it up. It had no training wheels, which didn't bother Troy at all. He took it to the top of the little hill that composed the back yard. He would mount, push, and off he'd go! What a thrill! Even hitting the fence and falling over had an element of excitement in it for Troy. He spent the entire afternoon flying down the incline, running into the fence, falling over, getting up and starting the entire process over. Maggie checked on him often, but couldn't stand to watch the whole time.

When Daddy arrived home that evening, a very excited little boy met him. "Daddy, Daddy, come see! I can ride my bike! Come see!"

Adam looked at Maggie, who smiled back and nodded. Together, they went out to the yard to watch. Jason was nearby, already having seen the display of joy and pride when he had arrived home from school.

Troy brought his bike over to the stretch of concrete that they called "the patio". Proudly, he got on the bike and rode it around the patio. He never fell or swerved. Adam was amazed. Troy had learned to ride a two-wheeler in a single afternoon! It wasn't long before Troy could ride around the neighborhood at neck breaking speed....

It was TammiBug, however, that had a laugh that would set the whole household laughing. It was absolutely contagious and charming! TammiBug was adorable, with her petite little body and curly hair. When she arrived, her hair was sparse, but as she enjoyed three meals a day, baths, shampoos, hair brushing and a great deal of general attention, it became thicker and maybe even curlier! She said the most outrageous things, and every event in her life, from breakfast to bedtime, was a celebration of life itself for her! Each day became a new celebration, a joyous event for all, seen through the eyes of this adorable, bright child. Not one member of the Taylor family could be around Tammi enough. They all adored her.

Spring turned into summer—and it was one of the happiest summers the family had ever shared. Adam laughed and laughed the day he came home and found all five of his other family members standing in a huge puddle of mud, covered with the goo from head to foot. Maggie had seen that puddle outside when she first woke up. She knew she had two choices ~ either try to keep cleaning up the mess each time the children went out to play (mud is a magnet for children!) or make it a fun time for all. So, she took the children out, and they ALL played in the mud! Never had they laughed so hard! Adam connected the hose to the hot water heater, draped it over the edge of the balcony, and turned it on. Maggie, Jason, Naomi, Troy and little Tammi were thoroughly hosed down before being allowed back into the house. And Adam had a story to tell everyone at work the next day!

There were opportunities to spend weekends up at the cabin, breathing in the fresh, clean mountain air and building camp fires where they could roast hotdogs, marshmallows and make s'mores. They enjoyed swimming trips—Troy sank like a rock, but that didn't daunt that child one little bit! The first time they took him to the pool, he walked to the edge and just kept on walking, as if he had never seen water before. Down he went, and Maggie and Adam almost panicked! They reached him, and never wandered far from their little daredevil. He never did learn to swim, but that was not a hindrance to his sense of adventure! Many a time either Maggie or Adam had to pull him, gasping for air, off the bottom of the pool! Tammi was a natural swimmer and loved the water as much as her brother...However, she tended to stay above water much more!

They enjoyed kite flying and home made ice cream. There were parties and jokes, and so much laughter. Even Naomi Joy seemed content for the first time in her life. These two children had worked a miracle in her heart!

Why is it that joy is so short lived? Maggie knew the saying; "Around every dark cloud there is a silver lining." Somehow, there must be an opposite truth—because it seemed that every joy carried with it the advent of pain. And so it would be with the adventure with Troy and Tammi, who had firmly become a part of their hearts.

Reconciliation

Maggie hated this waiting in the emergency room. It wasn't the first time she had rushed Adam to the hospital. The first time, Jason had only been three or four years old. She had dragged him out of bed, taken him over to a friend's house, dropped him off, and taken Adam into the hospital. He had a kidney stone, which after a day in the hospital, simply disappeared.

There was the time he scratched his eye, and had to have it attended. He looked much different with that patch over his eye. The children said he must be a pirate!

But this time was the most serious. He had an upset stomach much of the day and evening. He had been vomiting as well. But when he started vomiting up blood....

They had hooked up his IV and she could hear them talking. She heard the words, "Intensive Care"...Could it really be that bad? Could he actually be in danger?

That week was formidable for the whole family. Adam stayed in the hospital for a long time with a bleeding ulcer. Maggie had a difficult time staying focused. Even when he got out of the hospital, a visiting nurse had to come in to teach him how to give himself shots and monitor him. He was now in serious danger of blood clots. Adam was sick for a long time...

About nine months before, Maggie and Adam agreed that it was time to start writing to his folks. Maggie had added them to her mailing list, a total of about thirty people each month. Perhaps they never read the letters, just threw them away unopened. None-the-less, Maggie wrote each month.

This month Maggie included the trauma of Adam's "close call". One thing she learned was that she must not take this man for granted! Life is fragile and not one of us knows when it will end. She wrote words of encouragement to each of the women on her mailing list, to take time to enjoy their loved ones, let them know how dear they are, and not to wait until it is too late. We need to honor our loved ones now. It would be much better to give flowers to one who can appreciate them now, than to their grave later...

There were few responses to the letter, but this was no surprise—there rarely was. However, one of them caught her by surprise. For the first time in six years, there was a letter from Adam's parents. Its message was simple; "I want to see you. You name the time and place." Thus ended six years of silence…

Adam and Maggie knew they had to be careful how they introduced the "new" children to Grandma and Grandpa. Grandpa, in particular, had a difficult time dealing with those around him who were not white. This very likely was part of the problem in the relationship before—with Naomi. Certainly not all, but some…

Maggie reflected on the time that she and Loreen were going through the grocery store when they passed a "mixed couple" and their numerous children. Maggie's eyes had lit up with pleasure as she looked on the beautiful little ones. "Oh, look at them all!" she quietly commented to Loreen.

Loreen kept her voice low as well, as she answered, "If you ever bring one of those *things* into our home, don't bother coming back again!"

Maggie had been taken quite aback. Now she wondered how in the world they were to let Mom and Dad know that they had two new grandchildren since their last visit six years ago. **And** that those grandchildren were half-black? They occasionally referred to them as their "chocolate" children, and God knew how they LOVED chocolate!

Maggie listened to Adam's side of the conversation as he spoke with his mother. They chatted for a moment and then Adam said, "By the way, Mom, would you believe you have two new grandchildren?" There didn't seem to be much of a response from the other side, as Adam continued to chitchat. After a bit, he commented, "By the way, Mom, the children…They are a little bit…dark…" Again, there seemed to be little response from the other side of the conversation. Mystified, Maggie just listened. After a bit more conversation, Adam said goodbye. Just before he hung up, Loreen had a question for him. Adam later laughingly told Maggie that last question was, "Ah, by the way, Adam, just how ahhhhhhh…*dark*…are these children?"

Adam's answer? "Pretty dark, Mom. Good bye!"

Maggie couldn't stop laughing. She hadn't laughed this hard since Troy and Tammi had gotten into an argument over which was correct in the song, "Jesus Loves Me" ~ "Jesus loves me 'cause I blow…" or "Jesus loves me in the snow…"! "Pretty dark", my eye!

Adam and Maggie made the decision to meet with his parents alone first. Adam was determined to protect Maggie and the children, even at the expense of his relationship with his extended family. During the visit, the conflict that had separated them was never mentioned. Both couples carefully skirted the issue and stayed with "safer" areas of discussion. In spite of the tension each of them felt at meeting after such a long separation, the time went by quickly. They set up a time for the family to visit as a whole. Jason was reserved, but Naomi, Troy and Tammi were delighted to go to Grandpa and Grandma's house to play and get acquainted. Naomi vaguely remembered her grandparents; Troy and Tammi were always up to anything new and exciting! Loreen and Gary seemed to accept the new grandchildren and watched them play, asking a few questions about the little ones; background and whether or not they would actually be adopted by the family. This was, indeed, the intention. They hoped to adopt them in just a few months, as a matter of fact.

But, it was not to be. At Christmas time, a time that should have been so joyous, little Troy and Tammi were returned to the home of their biological mother. All involved knew that it was a poor decision, but the judge wanted to give the mother "one more chance". Against the recommendation of the caseworkers, therapists and other professionals, the two children were returned to a place they did not know. Troy begged Maggie to hide them, to keep them from leaving. How could he understand? When he realized that he had no choice but to leave this home, he went out to the front porch, and threw himself down to the sidewalk below, spread eagle. Maggie stopped him, held him, cried with him. At five years of age, he wanted to die…

The weeks that followed were difficult. Such small things reminded the family of the children and they expected to hear Tammi's contagious laugh, or see Troy running through the house, completely forgetting that "running is for outside". Jason expressed his anger openly ~ he wanted to do physical damage to that judge. Naomi withdrew. She seemed to have left, leaving a shell behind. She wouldn't talk about her feelings…

Spring returned once again. In spite of the wounds of losing the children, new life could not be held back, would not be denied. Trees began to bud out. Flowers began to show their colors. And the Taylors began to talk of trying again. Perhaps as the season changed and the world thawed out, so too, the desire to nurture life was stirred up again in their hearts.

Maggie and Adam talked with the children about it. They would not put Jason and Naomi through this a second time ~ unless the whole family agreed, and the children in question were free for adoption. Jason agreed. Naomi rejoiced. She wanted a little sister again. And she seemed to do so well with a little one around. Perhaps it was time to start over.

May, 1990

Having a toddler around after such a long time certainly presented some new challenges. Little Ruth was such a happy go lucky child, unlike her brother, Paul, who was two years older. Ruth was quickly nicknamed "Sunshine"! Maggie would sing "You Are My Sunshine" to her on a regular basis. But, she wisely kept a constant eye on her. The baby was curious about everything, into everything and all over the place. Nothing was safe from her little fingers.

One day as Naomi was practicing her accordion; little Ruth toddled into the bedroom with a "treasure" of some sort clenched in her chubby little hand. Naomi glanced up and smiled. Ruth saw that smile as an invitation to join her big sister and happily walked over, hand extended. Ruth smiled in return and said, "Present?".

"A present for me? Thank you, Ruth!" Naomi extended her own open hand to receive the "present" Ruth had brought. When it was dropped into her hand, Naomi realized in horror that the gift had come out of the cat's litter box! As she shook out her hand, the only sound that came out of her mouth was a squeak.

It took Naomi only a moment to react. She scooped up Ruth, realizing that traces of her past activity were all over her face, hands, and clothes. Naomi quickly escorted her little sister to Maggie.

"Here, Mom, you take care of Ruth and I'll go check the bathroom."

Maggie took one look at Ruth and went to fill the bathtub in the main bathroom. In no time at all she had a fresh and clean, sweet smelling toddler and a bathtub that might take a week to clean out.

After cleaning up and popping Ruth into her crib, Maggie went to rescue poor Naomi, working hard in the downstairs bathroom. Indeed, Ruth had been busy. There were traces of her experimentation on the shower walls, bathroom walls, floor, toilet and sink, not to mention what the litter box looked like! Naomi, bless her, was scrubbing away with great industry at the walls. Maggie got another sponge from beneath the sink and joined her oldest daughter.

"Thanks, Mom. This is pretty gross."

Maggie laughed at the understatement and asked Naomi what had happened. As she listened, Maggie had to laugh. She laughed until tears ran down her face.

Naomi failed to see the humor ~ Maggie could only see the irony. This child, who had been kicked out of four day care centers/preschools because of her bizarre behaviors, including eating the inedible, had been totally grossed out by just such an item! It was just too funny.

Later, Maggie was on the phone, laughing as she related the story to her husband. When she said, "Oh, Adam, it was so funny!", she heard a disgruntled response from the living room. "It wasn't *that* funny," came Naomi's final comment on the entire episode.

Maggie was grateful for Naomi's help. Many were the times when Maggie would call Naomi and ask her to keep on eye on Ruth so that she could cook dinner. Naomi loved little Ruth, in spite of the child's hyperactivity, and enjoyed caring for her. She came up with games, taught her songs, helped her "color", and encouraged her language. Naomi had such a knack for caring for little ones. She seemed to have such compassion on young children. She seemed to know what would entertain them and how to keep them occupied. Often Paul would join in the fun, and Maggie would contentedly smile. Sometimes, life is good.

◆   ◆   ◆

Paul couldn't be more different from his little sister. Although he would participate in the fun times that the family shared, anger seemed to brew just under the surface. It rarely came out as the rage that seemed to be there, however. He was often sad but seemed unable to explain why to Maggie. She tried to encourage him to talk, but Paul simply wasn't interested. Instead, he "acted out" by soiling himself and his possessions, destroying his toys by shredding or dismantling them. Pulling one tiny thread at a time, he could unravel an entire blanket in a single night. His anger would occasionally erupt like the sudden explosion of an awaked volcano; yet the majority of the time it was expressed in quiet destruction of everything around him. Nothing was safe.

Somehow, in spite of these things, Maggie felt such a love for the wounded little boy. His big brown eyes and long eyelashes endured him to her. His fleeting smile could melt the hardest of hearts. On occasion, he could express such tenderness that Maggie could not help but be amazed. She loved to share quiet times of cuddling and reading with Paul. He was so quick, so bright. It was a joy to teach him even the simplest of things and watch his eager thirst for more.

He seemed, in particular, to be interested in the spiritual side of things. He loved to hear the Bible stories of great men and women. He could retell them, adding his own dramatic flourish to each story. Maggie saw, deep within this traumatized and hurting child, the glimmer of a pastor's heart.

Maggie called Ruth her "little Joy Bringer". Truly there was never a dull moment. Maybe she had given the name "Joy" to the wrong child! There was that one evening…

"Are you finished eating, Ruth?" asked Maggie after the little one had finished dinner. It was still difficult to keep her at the table if she was finished eating. Every thing at the table became a toy to the child ~ the flat ware, plates, brussel-sprouts, anything she could reach from her little booster chair. Naomi sat on the other side of her, but even with Maggie on one side and Naomi on the other, Ruth was a handful. Her hyperactivity simply could not be ignored! Ruth was wearing her dinner once again, except for what she had shared with Maggie and Naomi. Naomi cherished her long hair, but it seemed an automatic target for Ruth's grubby little hands. Was that mashed potatoes in it tonight? No, they hadn't had mashed potatoes…Well, they hadn't been anyway. Now they were! While Naomi cleaned the dinner out of her hair, Maggie did her best to clean up Ruth. Once clean enough to touch, Ruth was lifted down and place on the floor.

It wasn't more than three minutes before Ruth was back, tugging at Maggie's shirt. "Potty, see potty?"

"You used the potty, Ruth? Good girl! Show Mama!" Ruth was excited. She knew that an animal cracker or two was waiting for her! She took her mama's hand and led her in to the bathroom.

When Maggie entered the bathroom and made her mandatory check, she burst out laughing! She laughed until tears ran down her cheeks. Ruth wasn't too sure what to think of this odd behavior. Maggie pointed at the three brussel-sprouts in the little potty-chair. "Well, Love, now I know what you think of brus-selsprouts!" It was a long time before brusselsprouts would ever appear on the dinner menu of this household again!

When Ruth and Paul had been in the Taylor household for six months, a most amazing phone call came from the caseworker. Ruth was now almost two and a half. Her half brother was four. Naomi was finally ten and Jason a "true" teenager!

"Hello, Maggie?"

"Yes, this is Maggie."

"This is Beverly." Yes, Beverly, their caseworker. But this was an odd time for a call. It was not yet time for a visit…"How would you feel about taking in a newborn **Korean** baby?"

Beverly knew just where Maggie's soft spot was. Korean. Like Naomi. Was there any child as beautiful as an oriental child? And a newborn. Maggie and Adam never dreamed they would receive a newborn baby. A baby—untouched, undamaged, unharmed by the world. A baby. A **Korean** baby! It was all arranged—she and Adam would pick up the new baby the following morning, directly from the hospital!

Adam was more excited than Maggie was. And Naomi was more excited than either one of them! This baby would be her baby—Korean (well half-Korean—close enough!) like herself! The evening was a flurry of activity. Because Adam and Maggie had never anticipated receiving a newborn, they had nothing for a baby. The crib, of course, was there because Ruth had recently graduated out of it. They still had a crib sheet and a blanket as well. But that was it. Not a very grand start for a brand new baby!

It was so exciting! Arrangements had to be made. Naomi and Maggie went to borrow a cradle from a friend. It could be set up in Adam and Maggie's room until the baby would be old enough to move to the crib. They went next door where the neighbors had a new baby and borrowed a little sleeper in which to put the baby when she would come home.

Adam decided that, after picking up the baby, he would go shopping. Of course, they needed a front pack for going on walks, little tiny sleepers, new dresses, and diapers...In fact, he had the most crazy, wonderful idea. "I am going to have a baby shower! How about it? Other people have baby showers for their new babies. I think I'll have one—*Men only!*"

Maggie laughed. "Well, why not? You've wanted a baby girl for so long. Why not have a men's shower?" And so it would be—later! Right now, maybe they should pick out a name! They didn't discuss it for long. They wanted to name the baby after Maggie and her older sister. It was settled. Victoria after herself, Meghan Victoria; and Hope after her sister. Victoria Hope. They would call her Tori. They wouldn't tell anyone except Maggie's sister about the new baby and really surprise their friends at church on Sunday!

The following morning, Maggie and Adam went to the hospital and picked up the tiny little newborn, their Tori! The wait seemed to go on forever, but finally the nurse and social worker came to get them. The first thing they did was take her out of the hospital clothes and put her in the little sleeper they had borrowed. Tori had all her toes, all her fingers, but absolutely no hair at all! But, she was theirs!

The social worker, in combination with Beverly, related the story. This mother came into the hospital and, as she was delivering her baby, told the nurse that she wanted to put the baby up for adoption, but had not made any arrangements. Usually when this happens, the social worker would call specific agencies with whom she worked. However, "for some reason", this time she called Beverly. And Beverly knew just the home. Since she had no Asian parents on the waiting list, she would put the baby in a home with a Korean sibling. And that home "just happened to be" Adam and Maggie's! Adam and Maggie exchanged glances. This was not just "one of those things"; this was orchestrated just for them, just for Tori! Great things were in the future for this little one! Victoria—"victory". Hope—it was the perfect name!

Much excitement met the three when they arrived home. Everyone wanted to hold this new addition, and it was difficult to surrender her to the siblings. But, Maggie was able to do so and Adam took a whole roll of film as each sibling held their new little sister!

Indeed, Tori created quite a stir in church that Sunday! Everyone had a comment to make. "What a speedy pregnancy!" "I didn't even know you were expecting!" "Whose baby is this?" "How long will you get to keep her?" Naomi proudly showed off "her" baby—with comment on how much she resembled her big sister! Naomi basked in the attention as all the other young ladies came to see the baby, wanting to hold her, touch her, just sit next to her!

After church, a friend approached them. "I believe that this baby is a gift to you. You will have many challenging days ahead of you. But the Lord has given you this gift as a comfort-bringer ~ a source of comfort, to remind you that, no matter how difficult the times ahead, you shall have deep comfort in this child. Remember, God has not abandoned you, but has sent you a gift of love."

Maggie listening, convinced that those dark days were behind them, NOT ahead of them. Life was so good now. Surely, they had been through the "valley of the shadow of death" ~ only life lay ahead! This same word, however was spoken twice more over the following week. She should have known that she should prepare for a trip up a bigger mountain than they had yet encountered…

Six glorious months passed—the baby became a bond between the older children and the younger, a common focus. It seemed to pull the family so much closer. Naomi loved holding her, talking to her, and encouraging her. Tori seemed to grow so quickly—she was full of laughter and fun.

How could it be that Maggie missed the undercurrents? As she reflected back, there were some odd things, but she hadn't really focused a lot on them because things at home seemed so good. Why couldn't she just enjoy that and let the school worry about the school hours and issues?

There had been a major change in the school—a new principal who really seemed to care about Jason and Naomi, was making a great difference. He was willing to stay in touch with the family, calling, sharing, and talking about how things were going. He was curious about Naomi; she seemed to have two totally different sides to her personality. Sometimes he wondered if she had two different sides of the same personality—or two distinct personalities?

Maggie had often wondered that in the past—it seemed that TWO people lived in that body, Naomi, and Naomi Joy. One was the cooperative, eager to help girl of joy. The other was angry and hurtful. The stealing was out of control. There was vandalism now. And it was "the other one" that was playing with Ruth the day Ruth had been jumping on Naomi's bed and had "fallen" into the dresser. That accident resulted in a trip to the hospital—Ruth received stitches where she had actually bitten all the way through her bottom lip. Stitching her up, and later, taking the stitches out, was a horrible experience for all involved.

Another time, Naomi was helping little Ruth take a bath. Somehow, Ruth "fell" again—this time chipping one of her front teeth. There were other "accidents" as well, to the point Adam and Maggie kept a pretty close eye on the relationship, just in case the accidents weren't really accidents…Yet, most of the time now, Naomi was so helpful, caring, loving…Besides, don't ALL teenagers have some mood swings; some outbursts of anger; some rebellion? Wasn't this just part of growing up??? Maggie had never heard of a child that became so angry, she hit herself with a hard earned trophy until she bruised her own face, but maybe this was a part of some of that process…

At school, other things were going on. Many were matters of manipulation. On occasion, Naomi would meet a friend at the door of the school. "I put the gift on your desk. You are going to really like it! Wait 'til you see it! Did you bring the candy (or make up, or whatever…)".

After giving Naomi the agreed upon item, the friend would go to her desk and find—nothing. Of course, Naomi was all innocence. Of course, someone else must have come by and stolen it. How dare they? She would be properly indignant, even outraged. And Naomi would get the item she wanted—though her friend would never see what she had negotiated to receive!

Another time, Naomi arranged with a friend to run away from home after school. They would meet at the large park in the middle of that part of town.

They worked out how they would have a supply of food, and where they could sleep. There were a number of sheltered areas ~ going to this park was like going to the mountains. They could hide there for a long time, Naomi's friend bringing in food as needed. The friend was very concerned about Naomi, it seems. Naomi shared tales of horrible things going on at home and the friend felt so badly for Naomi. How could she possibly endure such treatment? Why, Naomi even had bruises to show for it! Surely she would be better off hiding, with someone to supply her needs. At least for awhile.

The principal also shared those times when he wondered if Naomi really didn't know what was happening in her life. For instance, one time Naomi found a big pile of spit balls on her desk. She was furious! How did they get there? Who did that? Why would anyone do such a gross thing? And to her, of all people?

Yet, other students had SEEN Naomi make and stash those spitballs right where she found them! Her shock and righteous anger seemed genuine, however. She truly did not seem to know that she, herself, had placed them there!

Many other such incidents occurred—gym clothes flushed down the toilet, bathrooms flooded, mild acts of vandalism, all witnessed by others yet Naomi seemed totally surprised by each incident and shocked that anyone would say she was involved!

April 1992

The adoption date was set and only a few days away when that dreadful call came...

"Naomi told the other girls at school that the mark on her face is from being slapped—by you."...

"I just wanted to let you know...And see if there's anything I can do. Do you need help or anything? Are the children giving you a bad time? I can understand frustration, maybe even to pushing Ruth down the stairs, but..."...

"Naomi said, well, that you pushed Ruth down the stairs, and now she is afraid to go down them at all...I was worried..."...

"...Does little Tori have a burn on her hand?"

Maggie sat down hard in the nearby chair. "Oh, my God. Oh, my God."

"Maggie, are you all right?"

Maggie's voice was barely audible. She whispered, "Yes, but it was an accident. Jason set her right next to a hot casserole dish on the table. He didn't mean to hurt her! It was only an accident. He wouldn't hurt Tori for the world!"

Candy's voice was quiet. "Naomi didn't say anything about Jason, Maggie."

Understanding slowly seeped into every part of Maggie's being. "Why would she do this? Why would she say these things? Surely no one would believe this!"

"I'm afraid a lot of people believe it, Maggie. I don't know how far it has gone—how far it will go. But I thought you should know." There weren't many words of comfort Candy could offer—and even having heard denial from Maggie's mouth didn't totally convince her it wasn't true. People can do some strange things under stress. And Naomi sounded so convincing. But, she had known Maggie a long time, and she sure didn't seem the sort—although she didn't know for sure what "the sort" was. They talked for a bit longer, then Candy had to go.

Maggie stayed in the chair for a long time, tears running down her face. She tried so hard to love this child. Naomi, why do you do these things? How much pain will you inflict? Where will it end? Who has heard? Have my other friends heard this—and do they believe it? Why would they even think I could...Sobs broke out....I could burn my own baby? Burn her?! Never! And push little Ruth down the stairs? Oh my God, help me! What will I say to her? How can I respond. It hurts, oh it hurts, it hurts...Rocking back and forth, hugging her arms close, Maggie sat and cried. Oh, God, just take me now! Let me die! Just take me now! I can take no more...no more...

Jason, Naomi and their father were out for awhile. Six month old Tori and two-year-old Ruth were both sleeping in the room they shared. Paul, almost five years old now, was in his room and quiet for the time being. Maggie thought—somehow she would need to respond to Naomi when she returned from her band class. She and Jason were playing in the same band, so they would return together soon. What will I say? How can I deal with this? I don't know how to talk to Naomi about this. We've had a hard time since she came—but how do I take care of this situation? She wished there were someone she could talk to about this, but who would really understand? The tears kept coming, but there seemed to be no answers.

By the time Jason, Naomi and Adam arrived home, Maggie had tenuous control over herself. It was obvious that she had been crying, in spite of having run cold water over her face and spending some time trying to "get it back together". She had spent time crying out to the Lord, praying, thinking and trying to plan how to deal with this new situation. There had been no accusations like this since they had first moved to Denver. But this was *much* worse. This was initiated purposefully by Naomi. The lies were finally going to injure the entire family.

Maggie waited until Adam was in the house, the last of the family to enter. Then she suggested Jason go get ready for bed, but she wanted to talk with Naomi and Adam before Naomi followed suit.

"Naomi, I received a phone call while you were gone. It seems some people are believing that I have hurt you, little Ruth and Tori."

Naomi looked back at her mother calmly. "Oh? That's interesting..."

"Naomi, this person said that you informed them that I hurt them—that I pushed Ruth down the stairs—and purposely burned Tori!" Already the pain was creeping back into Maggie's voice.

"Strange. I wonder where they would get an idea like that..." Naomi failed to react to Maggie's words. Maggie could see, however, the absolute shock on Adam's face.

"She said that you told them at the school that I have been hurting the children; that I hurt you. The students have been telling their parents, and..." a sob involuntarily escaped her, "and they believe it. MY friends actually believe I am hurting my children! How could you do this, Naomi? Why would you do this?" Maggie was losing any control she had hoped to have. She was crying now. "They will ALL believe you! Because of you, even my adult friends will turn away! How could you hurt me like this? Why, Naomi, WHY???"

Naomi seemed unaffected. There was simply no reaction. She simply shrugged.

Maggie couldn't stand it. "Have you NOTHING to say? NOTHING???"

Adam interrupted. "Wait a minute. Tell me what happened. Let's try to figure this out, okay?"

Maggie took a deep breath and tried to steady her hysteria. Adam offered his handkerchief and Maggie wiped her eyes before blowing her nose noisily. Then she tried to explain the phone call, leaving out the name of her concerned friend. She concluded by saying, "She really believed it, Adam! She really believes it! How many others believe it? How many other parents will be shunning us, believing that we would do these things? Oh, God, Adam! Its been so hard before; but now.... What are we going to do? How can I even show my face at church? What are we going to do???"

Adam knew there were no concrete answers. There was nothing he could say to comfort this terrified, tormented woman. He remembered that day so long ago, when they sat outside the office of the agency from which they had adopted Naomi. This moment held the same deep, unspeakable pain. He was overwhelmed by the same sense of hopelessness. But, they had gotten through that appalling trauma. Surely, this too, would be overcome. He held his wife, murmured into her aching soul, and prayed.

Naomi was no longer unaffected. She, too, had begun to cry. Those words that so rarely were spoken sincerely from her lips were barely audible. "I'm sorry, Mom."

There are times that pain is corrupted into anger, even rage. Maggie had been to that edge many times. There had been times that she had even crossed the line, struggling intensely with the guilt and shame afterwards. But never had she hurt this deeply. Never had she wanted to hurt another so much. She turned to her daughter, eyes flashing through the tears. "Isn't it just a little bit late for that now? I…" How many times had she choked back the words before? How many times had she denied the emotions buried so deeply within her? She gasped that awful word, "…hate…" It was out, never to be snatched back when sanity returned. "…you."

Silence, except for the sobs racking Maggie's body. Shock creased Adam's face. The color drained from Naomi's. She had pushed her mother past the point that she had ever pushed before. And Maggie had finally spoken the words Naomi knew she would one day hear. Yes. She knew that she would be rejected once again. Just as her birthmother had rejected her. Just as her birth family had rejected her and sent her far, far away. She had known, deep down, buried somewhere in the depth of her very being, the silent part that even she had never truly understood or even been aware was there, that someday this woman, too, would reject her. The word rang through her soul; captured, amplified in her ears. Hate. It was imprinted deeply in her mind. Naomi turned and went downstairs to her room. Without knowing it, she had believed it. The turmoil inside had finally been solidified into a word. "Hate".

Naomi did not see her father sadly rocking her mother. She did not see the tears on his suddenly old cheeks. She did not hear her mother sob in the gathering darkness, "Oh, God, what have I done? How can I still love her when I hate her so much?" And there were no answers.

The Investigation

Maggie decided that she had better run to the school early to deliver some paper-work before picking up the children. She was surprised to see the caseworker in the hallway. Strange. Though some other families in the church were now adopt-ing, they had different caseworkers. As far as Maggie knew the <u>only</u> family with whom Beverly was involved was their own.

"Good afternoon, Beverly. Imagine meeting you here, of all places!" Maggie feigned a smiled, in spite of a growing uneasiness.

Beverly returned the smile. "Yes, I didn't expect to see you either…"

Maggie scrutinized the woman. She could discern nothing. "May I help you. Are you looking for someone in particular?"

"Well, as a matter of fact, I want to meet with the principal. I need to speak with your children."

Ahhhhhh. Of course. Maggie made the connection between the painful reve-lation of the Naomi's lies and the presence of the caseworker. "Oh, sure. I can help you there. Let me go get him for you." The cover was likely flimsy. But at least she could get the chance to tell the principal what was going on ~ and to please not allow the caseworker to be alone with the children. There was no doubt in Maggie's mind that SHE would be politely asked to not be present! Quickly it was arranged. He was happy to sit in and try to get a clear picture of what was going on.

Maggie prayed while the parties met together. It was no coincidence that Maggie walked in the door just in time to see Beverly in her search. Naomi and Jason were questioned separately ~ each time with the principal present. After-wards, Maggie was informed that the adoption was now on hold until the com-pletion of "The Investigation." With that, Beverly was gone.

The principal, Mr. Myers, met with Naomi afterwards. He said both children had answered the caseworker's questions simply. Naomi told the caseworker how Maggie had gotten upset with Ruth because Ruth refused to clean her room up before dinner. Maggie had gone to check the room and when Ruth refused to comply, she "pushed her down the stairs". The marks, now faded, on her own face were where Maggie had slapped her "for no good reason". If she wanted to know if the marks had, indeed, been there, Beverly could ask several of Naomi's friends who would be more than happy to validate her story. And, yes, Maggie had purposely burned the baby.

Jason had told Beverly that <u>he</u> was the one responsible for Tori's little burn—and that the doctor had already seen it as they had been in to see him on a routine check up the following day. The pediatrician had assured them that it was minor and he was not concerned about it. He had no recollection of Ruth's being pushed down the stairs. She was afraid of stairs, as well as dogs, cats, squirrels, beetles, spiders and flies! Besides, how could Maggie check Ruth's room and then push the child downstairs? Ruth's bedroom WAS downstairs! Finally, Naomi had gotten a trophy the preceding summer at the accordion contest. When she was angry one day, she had hit herself with the trophy. It wasn't uncommon for Naomi to hurt herself—she had done that since she was little!

Beverly had even interviewed Mr. Myers, and he had been able to support Jason's remarks. He had seen some of these things himself. They had similar things happen at the school on a fairly frequent basis. The question now was, what would happen next.

There were several possibilities. The worse scenario would be that the Department of Social Services would take Maggie to court for child abuse and they would lose all the children. At best, the adoption date would be delayed until The Investigation was completed and all possible charges dropped. All the could do now was wait—and pray…

It seemed that there were additional "concerns"; reported by an unknown person. When the lawyer called, he informed Maggie and Adam that they were working through those now. It seems that Adam was the brunt of some of those ~ abandoning Maggie and the children on several occasions as well as physically abusing the children and his wife! Maggie was amazed how this thing was snowballing, and Adam was shocked at the accusations. Where in the world would they be coming from? Why would anyone think, and even worse, <u>say</u> that he would abandon his family? And when, exactly, had he ever abused his children? Or beaten his wife? By law, the accuser was protected; they need not come forward. Adam was furious. They had dealt with this before, years ago. Was it not his constitutional right to face his accuser?

Maggie met with her friend, telling her what had happened. Connie was sympathetic, having received her own "sibling group" as foster children at the same time Maggie and Adam had received Paul and Ruth. In fact their adoption dates were within days of each other. After pouring out her heart, Maggie bowed her head while Connie prayed. She asked the Lord to reveal the accuser, that he or she would be unable to sleep or eat until they came forward and faced Maggie with the accusations that had been reported. Connie sincerely believed the Lord would answer this prayer. Maggie was skeptical. Of course, Connie wasn't as familiar with "The System" as she herself was. She didn't know any better...

It was only a few days later that Maggie received the most amazing call. "Maggie, I have to confess that I have been unable to eat or sleep for the past week..."

Stunned, all Maggie could do was listen! This was a friend with whom she had been working as members of the board of directors for a private placement organization. They worked together to help place children in Christian homes. Maggie had made some innocent comments, and Jenny has misconstrued the meaning. Jenny's husband was the lawyer for the adoption process. When he had asked her, after getting the report of Naomi's accusations, if Jenny had ever heard anything from Maggie that seemed suspicious, Jenny recalled a number of statements. Jenny wondered if, perhaps, they could meet together, just the two of them to clarify some of those statements. They arranged to meet for lunch the following day.

Maggie was nervous about meeting with Jenny, knowing that Jenny had reported, through her husband, to social services, a number of accusations. How could she defend herself? Should she even try? Maybe she should just give up. She wanted children so badly. She loved children and knew that she could offer them something special, deep. Yet, it seemed that these doors kept getting slammed in her face—and the pain was almost unendurable! Why did she have to care so much? What would she say???

Maggie knew she had to call Connie and let her know that her prayer had been answered ~ and that it was their lawyer who was working **against** them! In fact, this lawyer was also the lawyer for Connie and her family, in their own adoption process! Connie was thrilled that her prayer had been answered so precisely, so quickly! It was, of course, disconcerting to find out that it was their own lawyer bringing these charges, but if God was in control, what would this "little" issue change?

Jenny was already there when Maggie arrived at the restaurant. Apparently, Jenny had reached their meeting place early so she could secure a table. Maggie sat down and faced her "friend".

It seemed that Maggie had made two comments to Jenny that had grossly mislead the woman into thinking that Adam was not the faithful husband he claimed to be. Why had Maggie stated that she "had to hurry back home (after a meeting) because she was concerned about leaving Adam home alone with the children for too long"? On one occasion, Maggie had also asked for Jenny to pray for her as she was a "single mom again, for awhile…".

How could such simple statements become such major issues? Maggie explained that Adam's health was not all it could be, and he had just gotten out of the hospital. It was difficult for him to stay on top of things at home for very long, but he had agreed that Maggie could still attend that meeting with Jenny. Maggie wanted to relieve him of the responsibility of five children as early as possible so he could rest!

As to being a "single mom", Adam was NOT abandoning his family on a regular basis! He was in a position with his job that required out of town trips on occasion. A little extra prayer helped those times with the children go more smoothly!

Jenny was relieved to hear those explanations and told Maggie that she would share that with her husband, and see if the adoptions could be finalized.

Later that week, Adam did hear from their lawyer, who now felt comfortable with allowing the legal adoptions to proceed. In the meantime, Maggie and Adam had decided to find a new lawyer, thank you very much! They were able to adopt all three little ones on April 30th—only three weeks after their original court date.

Again...

How could things ever be the same between Maggie and Naomi again? Maggie could apologize to Naomi for the things she had said, but words can not be taken back once spoken. The damage is done, the pain inflicted. Maggie reflected on the fact that an apology from her was, none the less, necessary, knowing full well that an apology from her daughter would never come. However, she had to try to make amends, regardless of how Naomi may or may not respond. How often are we willing to justify our behavior by the lack of appropriate response of another? This must not be the case. She had to do what she knew was right, no matter what others decided to do...Sometimes, she thought, I get tired of "doing the right thing"...

Life did calm down for awhile again, back into a routine. The tension remained, Maggie was always waiting for what might be coming, and Naomi, anticipating further rejection, seeking it out. The stealing, lying, vandalism and self-abuse continued. Maggie wondered if things would ever change. She was so grateful for Ruth, her little joy-bringer; and Tori, her comfort bringer. She needed both—joy and comfort!

Maggie had started meeting with one of the elder's wives at the church. Maggie had learned to trust the wisdom and compassion of Phoebe and shared her own sense of discouragement and defeat. Phoebe was interested in learning more about this "Reactive Attachment Disorder" and encouraged Maggie to share her experiences as well as gather additional information and research concerning the disorder. Maggie was grateful for the organization in a small mountain town near Denver where research was being done. She sent for all kinds of materials, which she shared with Phoebe.

Phoebe asked if she could share the information with her husband, Don. Don and Phoebe had always been supportive of Maggie and Adam, and Maggie was more than happy to help this caring couple to learn more about a disorder that affected Naomi and the whole family so dramatically.

Maggie felt that Phoebe was truly beginning to understand, to empathize with her, more clearly the reason Naomi struggled and did some of the "unusual" things she tended to do. With Naomi attending the school where Phoebe taught, perhaps Phoebe could observe some of those behaviors and understand the cause behind them.

One session, Phoebe let Maggie know that she felt it was time to meet together as couples, Don and Phoebe with Adam and Maggie. Don felt he had some wisdom to share with them, as a couple.

The evening was cool, so Maggie wrapped the baby in a soft, warm blanket. Tori was such a cuddly baby and wrapped up tightly, she was a delight to hold. Maggie was optimistic as Adam drove them across town. It felt good to have someone to talk with, someone with experience that could be shared. Adam seemed nervous, though Maggie had assured him that this was simply a meeting to help them deal with the seemingly never ending battle. He just felt uncomfortable with the whole idea of meeting with Don and Phoebe.

Things went terribly wrong from the very beginning. Don made it very clear that he did not believe in the "false diagnosis" of a lack of attachment on Naomi's part. All he could see was a man who refused to take "spiritual leadership" of his family, leaving his wife and children to flounder in the world. It was not surprising that the thin rope of hope had led Maggie astray! She needed something to which she could cling, but was instead being hung by that same, deceptive rope! According to Don, every problem poor Naomi had could be directly attributed to Adam's grossly inadequate leadership!

Adam was absolutely shattered. Maggie was in tears. Both felt such a sense of betrayal and abandonment. How could someone for whom they had so much respect more completely annihilate their lives and faith? Surely the pastor must not be aware of Don's stand. Yet Don assured them that he spoke the opinion of the church leadership! Could this be true? Did they truly believe that Adam was responsible for the dysfunction in their daughter's life? How could they ever trust these people again? Were they speaking from the wisdom of God? And could Adam ever recover from such an unexpected and vehement attack? Maggie looked at him through her tears and doubted that she would ever see Adam whole again…

Maggie reflected back on Naomi's baby and toddler-hood. Someone had once told her that adolescence was simply a larger version of a child's toddler-hood. Funny. But, it seemed to be true! The screaming was different now, of course. Unfortunately, Maggie was doing as much of the screaming as Naomi was! It seemed that any calm they had found in the past was just that—past.

There were times that Maggie felt that she and Naomi were best friends. They could care for babies that came into their home as foster babies; working together and sharing the joys of such little ones. They could go for walks and enjoy one another's company. There were times of such closeness.

Then, it seemed that the next moment, they were screaming at each other. They fought over so many things, Naomi accusing Maggie of stealing her clothes, jewelry, diaries; Maggie was furious when Naomi went shoplifting or any number of other things. It brought tension between Maggie and Adam as well.

Counseling did not seem to be the answer. In fact, Adam and Maggie felt like they could recite by memory what the various therapist and counselors would tell them. They had been in marriage counseling for so long over the years, they should be qualified to <u>become</u> marriage counselors! Parenting classes were becoming old hat as well ~ in fact, Maggie and Adam <u>did</u> facilitate some classes on "Failure to Attach" children and how to work with the younger children. But what does one do when those young ones become teenagers?

There was no question that Naomi needed some help as well. They did find one therapist that claimed she worked with such young people with some success. Maggie and Adam decided that it might be worth a try. Naomi would have individual sessions as well as group work to do. Maggie watched as the other young people came in for group and cringed. Listening to them talk among themselves made her wonder how *this* could be helping. The language was crude, grating against her nerves. They had little, if any respect for the adults that brought them. Rather than Naomi improving, she feared that Naomi would become more like these other girls and problems could only increase.

Maggie was so excited! Her long time friend, Debbie and her family were coming to visit! How long had it been? Twelve years? More perhaps? Debbie moved from Utah the summer before Naomi came to join the Taylor family. They often talked about how nice it would be to have a daughter, much as they loved and adored their sons. Just when a daughter was arriving, Debbie and her family moved to New Mexico. It wasn't long after that, the Taylors moved back to Colorado. Though distance separated them, they remained best of friends. Maggie was filled with eager anticipation as she and Adam planned the things the families would do together. Jason remembered his friends, and helped with the planning.

Such a reunion! Maggie and Debbie hugged one another, laughing and crying, while Adam and Doug shook hands—as well as their heads, at the emotions of women. Adam was, none the less, pleased to see Doug after such a long time.

And how the three boys had grown! Of course, not only had Jason and Naomi grown, but also the family was considerably larger now! Between them, the two mothers went from having three children to parade around, to eight! Debbie was thrilled with the new "little ones", just as Maggie had known she would be.

The Phillips family would be staying for a full week, and the Taylors had planned far more than they could do. They had long ago learned that flexibility is the key to enjoying company.

They could just sit and chat, have a barbecue, take naps or go out and about. There are many things to see around Colorado ~ "God's country" Maggie called it!

Debbie and Maggie sat down that evening; just like "old times" over cups of specialty tea. Each had prepared to share their favorite teas, their latest discoveries, as they went over some ideas for their time together. There must be time for simple pleasures—walks in the early mornings or evenings; visits to parks where they could watch the children play; cups of tea with a bit of conversation; maybe a movie or two…Of course, a trip to the mountains was a must—as was a visit to the Garden of the Gods.

Maggie relished the opportunity to pour out her heart to her friend, and to hear Debbie share those things on her own heart. Maggie had so often felt alone in this struggle with Naomi. Few understood the confusion, pain, anger, bitterness, and loneliness. Other families saw only the inadequacies of the parents. Rejection, criticism and alienation seemed to be a constant in their lives. It was so good to have a friend that could listen and comfort, even though she could not understand. They spent hours together, laughing and crying; sharing their joys and sorrows.

Maggie reflected upon how truly blessed she was. Debbie had been her first true, close friend. Perhaps Debbie didn't have the shared experience of caring for an unattached child, but she was certainly willing to listen without condemnation. They stayed in touch all this time and Debbie had heard some of the stories. Now she could see for herself the amazing adventure of raising such a child. Not only Naomi, but now little Paul was showing more and more of the same kinds of behavior. Debbie was truly a sympathetic ear.

The morning of their excursion to the Garden of the Gods dawned gloriously. It was as if God wanted these visitors to see that Colorado could rival New Mexico for its sunshine! It promised to be a beautiful day, full of promise and light-hearted memories.

Both families were ready and, thanks to the roomy, twelve-passenger van, piled into the vehicle with much joking and laughter. It was only a short drive to The Garden and in no time they all tumbled out of the van to the spectacular sight of Kissing Camels and other remarkable formations. After a relatively brief visit to the souvenir shop/guest center, the Phillips and Taylors went out to hike, climb and enjoy the sights. They wanted pictures at Balanced Rock with all the children "holding up" the rock, a visit to the trading post, and a picnic lunch in one of the little areas set aside for that purpose.

The boys seemed determined to climb to the highest point, just to harass their mothers. The three Phillips boys and Jason helped young Paul to move among the rocks and walls, much to his unending delight. Paul was younger than these "big boys", but they tried to make him feel like a part of the group. He was amazingly agile and seemed to have little fear; so the height or difficulty of any of their antics did not intimidate him. He didn't know that the older boys were taking it a bit more carefully than they might have otherwise, which suited Maggie just fine. Of course, the daddies couldn't resist the challenge either, so they joined in with the boys. Naomi participated for awhile, but seemed satisfied to return to the "women" and play with the little girls. There seemed to be plenty to show the little ones ~ how to make daisy chains, necklaces out of the needles of the pine trees, gathering pretty rocks, walking barefoot in the grass. It was a contented time, restful and joyful. Yes, a memory to be tucked away and taken out now and then as a precious treasure of friendship. The two families returned home late in the afternoon, hot, sweaty, dusty, with not a few bumps and bruises, but happy!

It was a shame to leave their friends the next day to take Naomi to therapy. They had been working with the program for several months now, and Maggie didn't feel that it would be a good idea to cancel the appointment.

At the end of Naomi's appointment, the therapist called Maggie in to talk with her.

"I wanted to talk with you with Naomi here. She has a concern."

Maggie looked at Naomi. A concern, she thought to herself. She couldn't help remembering another such moment and feeling deep bitterness and resentment even before hearing the "concern". Somehow she knew something was coming that would disrupt their lives again in some very painful way.

"She tells me that her father became angry with her..."

Interesting. Most of the accusations had been against her personally. Now, Adam.

"...and grabbed her by the shoulder, leaving marks on her."

Ahhhh—marks on her. Interesting.

Maggie looked at Naomi again. No response.

"I thought it would be important to let you know before I take the necessary action. I assured Naomi that no one would hurt her for being honest and telling the truth."

Maggie answered, "Of course, Naomi wouldn't be hurt for telling the *truth*. We would do all we can to protect the truth of any situation…"

Maggie watched Naomi. Not a muscle moved.

"Well, good then. We do understand one another. We do want to be sure that Naomi feels safe and can come forth with these issues. I will, of course, have to report this to the proper authorities and wouldn't want anything else to happen. I am sure you wouldn't either…"

Naomi didn't say a word on the way back out to the car. Maggie was fuming. After everything they'd been through already, why couldn't Naomi figure out how much this was hurting them all? Wasn't it enough to hurt Maggie, without hurting every member of the family? And why was she doing this over and over?

"I just don't understand, Naomi! Why do you keep saying these things?" Maggie started to cry. Now she was mad at herself for crying—again—in front of Naomi. It just seemed to add fuel to the fire.

Ronnie, the investigator from Social Services showed up at the door the next day. Maggie recognized him immediately, and it was difficult to maintain her composure. She knew why he was there, of course, but did he HAVE to come when the Phillips were there?

Ronnie informed Maggie and Adam that a report had been received that Adam had left a bruise on Naomi's shoulder and that when he spanked Paul two days before, it had resulted in a bruise. Maggie was astounded! Paul? A bruise? A spanking? What in the world was THIS about?

He interviewed Adam, Maggie, Naomi, Jason and finally, Paul. Of the five of them, only one "remembered" the spanking. Not Paul, or Adam, but…Naomi. When questioned, Naomi said that Adam had been angry with Paul for soiling himself…*again*…and had spanked him. She had noticed it when Paul was taking his evening bath (though she didn't mention what she happened to be doing in the bathroom with Paul during his bath…)

Indeed, it was frustrating that Paul continued to soil and wet himself several times a day at the age of four. However, a bath and clean clothes seemed to be a healthier way to handle the problem than a spanking! Adam had not spanked the child, and suggested that Ronnie speak with the Phillips for confirmation of that ~ they had been present throughout the entire day, and most of the previous week as well! Ronnie felt this was unnecessary, but DID want to interview Paul "privately". Ronnie discovered that Paul did, indeed, have a bruise. Paul said he didn't remember how he got it—but that maybe it happened when he fell down at Garden of the Gods. Ronnie documented the information, and then even photographed the bruise for the records! All this without informing the parents...

Paul was thoroughly humiliated. Maggie and Adam were angry about the lack of concern and compassion for the little boy, or even the consideration of letting them know he was going to subject their son to such a demeaning process.

Ronnie let them know that he would let them know the results of the investigation at a later date. There was, after all, a report <u>and</u> a bruise! Little else was needed...The fact that there was not a single mark on Naomi was also duly noted...

Doug and Debbie watched and listened in amazement. They had never been witness to such a procedure before.

The only thing that the two families could recall that would have bruised Paul was one of the spills he took while climbing the previous day. He had not complained ~ but that would be in keeping with Paul's behavior. Like his older sister, Paul seemed to ignore pain.

It was interesting, sitting down with Debbie that evening, over a cup of tea, to discuss the event. Now Debbie could see what Maggie had been telling her over the last few years. She could clearly understand Maggie's frustration. Adam and Doug discussed the situation as well. Doug and Debbie would be happy to testify, if need be. If they could do anything at all...Adam and Maggie told them that it seemed to make little difference. Facts rarely seemed to sway the opinions of "The Powers That Be"...

What does one say to Naomi? More confrontation would lead only to more anger. More anger would lead to more reports. How many more times could the Taylors endure this? How could the other children endure the stress? What was the best course of action? How does one fight this kind of battle? It was as if Naomi had found a very effective method for "spanking" BOTH her parents!

Poor Adam was hopelessly devastated. This was the first time that allegations were aimed directly at him. He could not understand this change ~ it had been difficult to help Maggie through this same trauma. Now he faced the crushing sense of despair that he had seen before in his wife. Not only was he now utterly abandoned by his church, but also even his precious daughter had turned against him...

After the Phillips left for home, Maggie and Adam received word that the investigation would be dropped. However, the reports and results would remain in their file. Of course…Maggie decided that there would be no more therapy for this family. It was supposed to help, not make matter worse. Every time they sought help, it seemed the "help" led them deeper into a pit that had no way out.

And Again...

Maggie was tired. Adam was tired. Sometimes, it was just too much. Just the other day, young Paul had been chattering as Maggie drove him for his therapy appointment.

"Sometimes, she does stupid things. You know what I mean?"

It was mindless things. Constant chatter. "Hmmmm." Maggie replied, her mind wandering.

"Like last week. You know what she did?"

"Hmmmmmm."

He was going on and on..."So, I went outside and looked in her window. I knew she would get up in a minute. She wasn't _really_ dead..."

Maggie jerked herself back into the present. "What? I think I missed something. Why would you think she would be dead?"

"You know. Because of the belt. But I knew she didn't really pull it that tight. Do you think she was just trying to frighten me? That's what I think..."

"Were you frightened, Paul? What did she do that would frighten you? Can you tell me again...About the belt?"

Paul looked at Maggie closely. "Well..." He seemed to be trying to figure out where to start over. "Remember how mad she was about you going in her room? You threw away the stuff on the floor? Well, she was really mad, Mom. And she called me in her room and asked if I wanted to watch her kill herself."

Maggie was shocked. She'd heard the threat before. But Naomi had never involved anyone else in it. She usually just bluffed to get a reaction. "And then?"

"Well, she put the belt around her neck and pulled. Then she pretended to fall down dead. But I went outside and peeked in her window, and guess what?"

"What?"

"That's when she got up and looked around. I knew she wasn't dead. She just wanted to scare me..."

"And were you scared, Paul?"

"Nahhhhhh—I just thought it was stupid..."

Brother.

Fighting. Fighting again. Therapy obviously hadn't helped either one of them. Things were just spiraling downward. They changed churches awhile back. Although it had been helpful for Adam and Maggie, Naomi was unable to cope with the changes. They hoped that becoming involved in the youth group would help. At first it seemed this was true. Before long, it was evident that there were two separate youth groups here. One group was "on fire", excited about their faith and sharing it. The other group spent time talking about how terrible their parents were, how controlling the schools, and how they could retaliate against an authoritarian world. Naomi had talked with Maggie about it in one of those wonderful, far too rare moments of closeness. Naomi seemed concerned about it—yet she tended to associate mostly with the second group.

It was a relief when the "old" church they had attended split, and they were able to attend once again with their previous support group. It was more than a church, more than a support group. It was "family". The leadership that had so hurt the Taylor family would keep the building, and the splinter group would start over, new, like a breath of fresh freedom and renewal. It would become a healing place, not just for this pained and damaged family, but for many others who had also felt betrayed and wounded by past church experiences. It was a welcome change.

The small group meeting that the family attended was so supportive. A man and his wife for whom the Taylors had the utmost respect led it. When the stress in the family became so great it appeared Maggie might be on the verge of a breakdown, the entire group set aside a week for prayer and fasting. Each individual chose a day of that week to fast and encourage Adam and Maggie. Sometimes, Maggie even felt that maybe she wasn't crazy after all and that some people could still love her...

There continued to be times in which the family truly worked and played together. The camping trips, full of laughter, were the highlight of every summer. The company for which Adam worked had a recreational area where they could stay in a cabin, go ice-skating or snow tubing. Every season had its attraction there. In the winter, early in the morning, when Maggie came out of the cabin, the trees would be frosted with glaze, standing out against the blue of the Colorado sky. In the spring, they would often sit out on the covered porch, watching the hail rain down and watch the fabulous "light show" complete with magnificent sound effects of booming thunder! In the fall, the leaves of the mountain aspen were a wondrous display of gold.

The children loved going up to "their" cabin and relished every opportunity. Those were the closest times, the most peaceful times. Maggie and Adam were able to experience such a sense of "normalcy", peace, and calm. Naomi loved to share all the mountain wonders with the little girls, and the boys could always find another mountain to scale!

One day, they went over to Eagle Rock and played among the rock formations for hours. Maggie and Ruth went exploring for awhile. After some time, Maggie realized that she was hopelessly lost. The feeling of fear was almost overwhelming. She called for Adam, knowing that, with his weakening legs, he could not come for her. Adam was having increasing trouble with his legs as a result of radiation treatment at the age of eighteen. But perhaps he could honk his horn—or something! It was such a relief when Naomi heard the calls and came to the rescue. Maggie hugged her and told her how grateful she was to see her. Naomi led them back to the car with her infallible sense of direction. Never had Maggie been so grateful for this daughter!

They always had two traditional dinners when they visited the cabin. Adam made his "Famous Camping Goulash"—a delightful stove top dinner that had to be burned just a tiny bit on the bottom to truly *be* Adam's Famous Camping Goulash! The other included roasting hot dogs over the open fire or in the wood-burning stove, followed by a feast of roasted marshmallows! A better feast could not be found!

They would reminisce of past trips every time they went to the cabin. They remembered how Naomi came to have a single dimple in one cheek. She wasn't born that way! It wasn't long after the first investigation when Naomi was only two years old. She was fairly steady on her legs by then, but one day, when hurrying through the cabin, Naomi fell, right into a can sitting by the door. The black eye that child got from that episode was a real sight to see! Adam and Maggie made sure they got a picture of Naomi, with that "shiner", standing near the can, for the agency, should they feel the need to investigate the injury! Though nothing came of the incident legally, Naomi sported the sweetest little dimple on one cheek after that!

So many stories, so many joys and laughs! "The Cabin" simply was the best place to be! They had even celebrated Christmas there one year. Was that the year Jason had leaned on the wood burning stove? The nylon jacket he was wearing didn't fare well, particularly the sleeves!

This year the family went up to the cabin for the annual skating party, including an extra foster child that had joined them for a few months. Sometimes, it was good to watch the pleasure the foster children took in the smallest of things. Together, all the children played a simple game of ice hockey. Their lack of expertise on ice skates made the day most amusing for all. Even Maggie tried to balance on those blades, with little success!

Why was it that times of such pleasure seemed to lead to times of such stress? It was November. The Taylors were preparing for their twenty-second wedding anniversary, to be arriving in just a few days. November, in Colorado, often had very cold weather, with snow and ice and wind.

Maggie and Naomi were in conflict—again. Finally Maggie had enough and erupted. "Just go to bed. I don't care where! Sleep in the dog house for all I care!"

Naomi disappeared for a few moments and then reappeared, wearing her nightie and bathrobe. She unlocked the sliding glass door and prepared to step out.

Adam looked up from his newspaper. "Where in the world are you going?"

"Mom said I should sleep in the doghouse—and I am going outside!" She answered defiantly.

"Young lady, you turn around and get yourself to your bedroom! No one is sleeping outside in this cold!" He shook his head. Women. Sometimes he simply could not fathom their thinking process!

The next day started out much like most others. Naomi was off to school and Maggie was home with the "little ones" ~ Paul, Ruth and Tori. It was a fairly difficult day, for this day one of the foster children, a very troubled boy named Joseph, would be moving out and going into a group home. Maggie cried—she always did when one of "their" children moved on. It didn't matter that they were going somewhere their needs could be better met. Breaking ties simply was difficult and painful!

Joseph had brought much laughter into their home, but Naomi and Joseph simply struggled with one another. Usually foster children helped ease the tension, as each member of the family reached out to them. The family seemed more unified as a whole when they were working together to nurture hurting little ones. But it had been much different with Joseph. Though they enjoyed the laughter and fun times, there was also times of tremendous strife. It was obvious that Naomi was jealous of the relationship that Maggie was able to enjoy with Joseph. Perhaps because Joseph and Naomi were fairly close in age...Sometimes, however, Joseph struck out at Maggie, actually hitting and hurting her. Should Maggie respond, he would shout back, "There's not a thing you can do, and you know it! The department has your hands tied!" The triumph in his face and voice shone out when this confrontation took place. Maggie admitted that this was true—their hands, in terms of discipline, were tied. However, this unhealthy situation could not continue, and it was time for Joseph to move on...

The caseworker helped Maggie and Joseph to pack up his huge assortment of belongings. It took until almost 4:00 in the afternoon. Maggie allowed Joseph to take "his" cat with him ~ the one he had helped rescue from the sewer system. The group home agreed; Maggie and Joseph decided that Maggie would have to come by often to see both him, and the cat. When all was loaded, Maggie, Paul, Ruth, and Tori stood in the driveway, waving, until the van was out of sight.

Maggie looked at her watch and realized that Naomi had not come home from school. Strange. She should have come home an hour ago. Where in the world was she? Maggie went to the phone and called the school. The principal answered.

"I'm sorry to bother you this late in the day, but Naomi has not yet come home from school. Was there a reason for her to stay late of which I was unaware?"

"No, not at all. I am sure she is safe. Surely she'll show up soon." The principal sounded reassuring. Maybe Naomi had stopped off somewhere to...well...to...do...*something*. Maggie decided to wait another half-hour. By then, Adam would be home.

Adam did arrive home shortly thereafter. He was also concerned. "Let's call him back and find out if she left with someone else. Could that be?"

Maggie called again. The principal was still there. "Did she leave with someone else? Perhaps another friend?"

"Well, she was hanging around her friend. And her mom was here. Perhaps I should tell you that Naomi said you locked her outside last night, and made her sleep in the shed..."

"Last night? Slept outside? No way! In fact, that was HER choice and her father stopped her!"

The pause on the other end of the line was brief. "Hmmm—I thought as much. However, we do have a responsibility."

Maggie sank to the floor. "You've already reported it?"

"You're a teacher, Maggie. You know the policy—and the law."

"Why didn't you come to us first? If you suspected it was false, why did you report it before even talking to us?"

The principal didn't even hesitate this time. "You know the law, Maggie. I had no choice."

"No choice, my eye! You always have a choice! You know Naomi! You know how she does this! You most certainly had a choice!" Maggie was sick to death of this game. Naomi playing the system to "spank" her parents, then pretending such innocence! She had told Naomi the last time they went through this, that she would not fight it. She simply did not have the energy and no longer had the desire. If the Department wanted Naomi, well then...

"I am simply following the law, Maggie."

Maggie was fed up. She had never hung up on anyone before. Today she made an exception.

She turned to Adam. "You're not going to believe this, Adam."

Adam did believe it. Somehow he wasn't the least bit surprised. And he knew Maggie was serious about not fighting "The-Powers-That-Be" this time. However, they did need to find Naomi. They sat down and worked their way through the little phone directory of the school. They narrowed the possibilities down to two families. Maggie dialed the first number.

"Hello?"

Maggie wasn't too sure what she should say! "Hello. This is Maggie Taylor. We were wondering if our daughter, Naomi, came home today with your daughter."

"Oh, Maggie! Yes, your daughter is here with us. We were just in the bathroom, talking and cleaning up. I told her that I could understand a parent becoming upset with a child. I might even have the child go outside! But to lock her out in the cold?"

Maggie refused to let anger rule her words. "Excuse me—but no one locked her outside in the cold. I know that you are trying to help. I imagine that your motives are good. However, are you aware that abetting a runaway is a felony offense in this state?"

"Ahhhhhhhhh," the woman was obviously not expecting this turn of events. "We'll have her right home..." Click—the phone was quickly hung up.

It was less than fifteen minutes that a car pulled up in front of the house, Naomi stepped out, and the car sped off! A stormy Naomi entered the house. Maggie and Adam glanced up. From her stance, they deduced that it would be wise to let her start any conversation.

It was amazing how those gorgeous black eyes could snap when Naomi was angry. "I didn't WANT to come back!"

Adam looked so sad. "We deduced as much. The principal has already reported us for child abuse. Do you remember what we told you the last time we went through this?"

"I might and I might not! And maybe I don't even care!"

Adam shook his head while Maggie fumed. "We told you we wouldn't fight any more..."

"Good! Then don't!"

Maggie was right on the edge when she spoke up. "I think you'd better go to your room, now!", she said through clenched teeth.

With a flounce, Naomi turned and stomped down the stairs to her room. Maggie turned toward her husband. "I can't stand this any more! She drags us through this over and over! She seems to *enjoy* it!"

"It gives her a sense of control ~ and it should! This is the best and most effective way she has of 'spanking' us. We do something she doesn't like and she retaliates..."

"Well, no more! Do you hear me? *No more!*"

As Maggie stopped for a breath, Adam grabbed her, embracing her. "No more," he agreed.

Maggie continued to struggle against him, her fury seeming to feed on itself. "Maggie, stop. This will not help. She has won. Admit it."

"IT'S NOT FAIR, ADAM! IT'S JUST NOT FAIR!"

Now Adam shouted as well. "This is *not* about fair, Maggie! No, it isn't *fair!* Nothing about it has ever been *fair!* So, just stop it! I <u>said</u> that it is over—no more fighting for her! Do you hear me? No more!"

Spent, Maggie slumped against Adam. He held her and for the first time in a long time, cried with her...

No one slept much that night. Maggie kept thinking about what was coming up now. Should they just give up? Was it finally time? Should they continue to try? Adam didn't know the answers either. His heart ached for his daughter ~ and his wife. It was as if he had to choose between two loves: the love he had for his daughter vs. that for his wife. What kind of a position was this in which to place a man, a husband...a father?

In the morning, Maggie heard Naomi coming up the stairs as she put breakfast on the table for the children. Their little heads turned as Maggie glanced up at Naomi. Naomi had her backpack and seemed ready to go to school. She was obviously still angry. "Just wait," she said as she looked at her younger siblings. "I am going to tell the investigator things so that *none* of you stay here with mom! They'll come and take you *all* away!" With that, she marched out of the home, slamming the door behind her.

Maggie's mouth dropped open in shock. Paul burst into tears. Ruth turned to her mother. "Where will I go, Mama? Who will I live with?" Her little chin quavered, her eyes tearing. Little Tori stared at the door and joined the other two in their crying.

"Now, now, babies! You are my babies! You are right where you belong and we'll watch after you. No one is coming for you." She comforted each of them, hoping they wouldn't detect the concern in her own voice. In truth, she knew that she was unable to protect the children; she had been involved with "The System" long enough to know that! She knew that Naomi would be resolute in her threat and the children were in danger. What a horrific feeling, to know there is danger coming and being unable to stop it! Tears and prayers. Sometimes, that is all we have...

The expected call came two days later. Maggie hated the suspense, but recognized that the investigator saw the report as a low priority due to the previous false reports. The more time that passed by meant the lower the level of concern on the part of the investigator. In the meantime, life with Naomi was pure hell. She was antagonistic toward all the children when home, making threats and frightening them. Maggie felt like her hands were tied, and found herself yelling back. This was only intensifying a very bad situation. When the call finally came, it was almost a relief.

"Hello, Maggie. This is Jordon. We received another report. What would you like us to do?"

Maggie almost laughed. There was no longer even a question of investigation ~ simply the question of how they would like it handled. "What do *I* want you to do? That's a rather unusual question!" she quipped.

"I've been to your house enough times to know what is in your backyard, Maggie! If you are going to lock a child in the shed, you should at least build it first!"

Maggie smiled. "Yes, I suppose that *would* be better planning. You know what I'd really like to do? I'd like to get help for Naomi. I know that there isn't anything I can do for her now. I've tried everything I know, and now it is obvious that she doesn't want to be here. As long as that is the case..." She trailed off.

Jordon paused for a moment. "What kind of help?"

"She needs professional help. I'd like to see if there is a residential facility somewhere that she can enter that will include school and therapy. The home, school, and therapeutic intervention teem need to work closely together so there is open communication and a consistency in place at all times."

Over the past two years, Maggie and Adam had spent hours pouring over such resources available in the states. They had called many such organizations, requesting information. They had folders of information in their files ~ most resources were not feasible simply because of the cost. In order to obtain such help, the other members of the family would be neglected, or they would have to declare bankruptcy. They had called many of them, asking if there was some kind of financial help. All had yielded nothing.

Jordon considered Maggie's suggestion. "Let me make some phone calls. I'll let you know what I find out as soon as I can."

Jordon was true to his word. His call came several hours later. "We have several possibilities, but there is no space open in any of them. We can place her only if there is an emergency. She needs to be considered a 'threat to the safety of herself or others.' At this point, I don't believe we can say that. I will continue searching, but it doesn't look hopeful."

Maggie wanted to argue. There was surely *something, somewhere!* They had far more resources than the Taylors did as a private party. "I know you'll do your best…"

It was the next morning, the day of Maggie and Adam's twenty-second wedding anniversary, Maggie found "The Note". There was little question, as Maggie read it, that Naomi was now a "threat to the safety of…herself". It was clearly a suicide note. She called Jordon.

"I'd like you to listen to this, Jordon, and then tell me what you think…" she said.

After reading the note, the pause was brief before Jordon answered. "Yes, it sounds like we'd better act soon. I spoke with the hospital yesterday and they do have an 'emergency bed' available. I'll call them now…"

With a sigh, Maggie hung up and called Adam. *He might as well know now how we'll be spending our anniversary,* she thought. They were supposed to be at Bible study tonight, and maybe it was a good thing…After calling Adam, it became a matter of simply waiting.

It was a painfully long afternoon. Finally, Jordon called. "We have a bed for her. The intake worker will meet you, your husband, and Naomi at the Martin Skylar Center at 5:00."

Naomi had come home from school about an hour previously. Adam would be home in just a few moments. This would be the most difficult day of her life…She remembered a story Adam had once told her. It was about a dream that Naomi had one night, a long time ago. She could picture Naomi at the door of a big building. Adam was driving away, herself in the passenger seat; turning, waving good-bye, tears running down her cheeks…They were leaving Naomi there. Alone. Perhaps for a long, long time. They had done all they could do…

When Adam arrived home, Maggie filled him in. They agreed to tell Naomi together. Adam called her. "Naomi, you had a dream a long time ago. You say your mom and I were driving away, leaving you at the doorway of a big building. Do you remember telling me about that dream?"

Maggie looked at Adam in surprise. He was referring to the same dream she had recalled earlier.

"Yes, I remember." Her words were mild enough, but that 'tough guy' stance spoke something else…Adam continued without seeming to notice.

"I think this is that day. We know that we are unable to give you the kind of help you need. There is a place, however, where you may be able to get that help."

Naomi shrugged. "Yeah. Right. Where is this place?" Such sarcasm.

"It is on the other side of town."

"And when are we going there?"

Adam sighed. "Now. We'll be taking the little ones to the Lander's. We have Bible study there tonight, so we'll just pick them up there later…"

"Okay. Let's go." Naomi put on her 'who cares' face and walked out the door. Maggie gathered up the little ones, bundling them up against the cold and telling them that their big sister was going to a special hospital where there were doctors to help her. There just didn't seem to be a lot to say…

The intake process seemed to take forever, although it was only a couple of hours. Maggie had hoped that, somehow, there would be time to talk with Naomi. There were so many things to say. How did it finally come to this? Would Naomi think she was doing this out of anger, bitterness and spite? Would she understand that Adam and Maggie had not stopped loving her? They were NOT abandoning her. Maggie kept praying, "Please, Lord, don't let her think we are simply abandoning her. Please, Lord…" Maggie wept there, in that place that seemed so cold and antiseptic. The doctor's questions went on forever, probing at every aspect of their lives. He talked to Maggie and Adam as others checked Naomi into the ward. Finally, after a brief hug for their daughter, Maggie and Adam watched the big doors close, locking. Naomi was locked in—or were Maggie and Adam locked out?

Adam and Maggie were relieved to return to the Lander's home, where friends were waiting. Friends. These friends would pray with them, hold them, wipe their tears, listen and comfort in the broken days, months, and yes, years ahead. Life would never again be the same. Would they ever be whole again?

March 25, 1996—A Letter of Love

Maggie sat at the table for a long time. What does one say to one's daughter who has desperately hurt the family, who lives with someone else, who is celebrating her birthday and who is still deeply loved? How could she communicate to Naomi the grace that God has for her, the way He had consistently watched out for her, the miracles she had been involved in, and the deep, deep love her mother had for her? Truly, life was different now. The house was calmer, more peaceful. Yet, there was an emptiness there, and in Maggie's heart. Certainly there could be no question that Naomi was happier. It was obvious that the children were doing better. And, Maggie had to admit to herself, her own turmoil had finally come to a point of calm. Yet, what can kill a mother's love? Can anything? There was pain in Maggie's eyes as she took up her pen and started the letter. Parts of it bore tearstains when it was finished. Perhaps it could communicate to Naomi something that Maggie had never put into words before.

Dear Naomi,

It is hard for me to believe that you are fifteen years old now! Daddy and I were talking this evening about a class he's going to be teaching soon, dealing with the gift of faith, gift of miracles, and gift of healing. We were coming up with experiences from our own lives that reflect the operation of these gifts to be used as examples. It is amazing to me to reflect on the huge number of miracles and healings we have personally received in our family, as well as the gift of faith God has blessed me with so many times in the past.

Have you watched your new <u>Carman</u> video, yet? Remember when he says that faith and fear are opposite extremes of the same thing? Fear is the belief that the worst will happen and faith is the belief that the best will happen. Hebrews 11 says that faith is the confident assurance that something we want is going to happen. It is the certainty that what we hope for is waiting for us, even though we cannot see it up ahead. It is like when Daddy had that bleeding ulcer and was in critical condition in the hospital. I knew, beyond a shadow of a doubt, that he was going to live. Same with when he had the brain tumor surgery. He could have died—I remember when one of the doctors was explaining to us what was going to happen. He said that one of the tubes he was placing in his chest had to do with preventing bubbles from traveling to his heart or lungs and killing him. It was scary, but I just knew he would live. I know that was a gift of faith from God. He gives me what I need when I need it.

It was like that with you from the very beginning. When we heard about you, we knew there was no way we could raise the money to bring you in from Korea. It was an awesome amount of money—thousands of dollars. But, we prayed and somehow God brought in every cent. One day we went to the mailbox, and there in the box were two checks, equaling a total of $400! That happened over and over—money coming from people all over the western states. One little boy had been saving up newspapers forever to raise money for his Scout troop. Instead, he sold them and gave the entire amount to us for you. One friend came to us one day and said that there was something they couldn't take with them on their move out of state. She wanted to know if we would take it. When we asked what it was, she answered, "our savings account." When the time came to pay each charge for your trip, paperwork, and adoption, the money was there, every time—to the exact cent! That should have been a clue as to what your life would be—a life of miracles and healing.

That was just the beginning of the miracles. There was the time you fell from that bunk bed. The doctors thought you had bleeding under your skull, the concussion was so bad. But tests showed differently—<u>before</u> they had to do surgery. There was the time your appendix burst, and by His grace, you lived through that. It was impossible, but you lived! So many other things happened, and God protected or healed you every time.

And now, you have reached your fifteenth birthday. Naomi, can you imagine what is in store for you? God has protected you so many times. Why? You are obviously very important to Him. I am excited to see what will happen as you mature. Congratulations on this birthday, Naomi. I love you.

Love,

Mom

As Maggie sealed the envelope, she wondered how such a letter would be received. Would Naomi read it? Would she be touched at all? Would she understand? Or would it simply go in the trash, unread? Would it be used once again to bring pain? She hesitated before she placed the stamp on the envelope. Should she even send it? So many questions. Always, so many questions. Maggie looked down at the letter. Slowly she turned it over, and over again. Perhaps the timing was wrong. Perhaps…Maggie put into her Bible. Maybe it would be better to just leave it there…The letter would not be sent. Not yet. Perhaps never.

August, 1997—A Final Letter

Adam held the newspaper in shock. He normally didn't read the "Legal Notices", but something led him to read them that day. There was a small notice that stated a young lady named "Naomi Joy Taylor" was changing her name to "Wendy Monique Cramer". Cramer? That was the last name of the foster family where Naomi currently lived. How many Naomi Joy Taylors could there be? This was <u>his</u> Naomi Joy! And she changed her name. She changed her name. He repeated it again. She changed her name. His mind simply could not comprehend the ramifications of this simple act. She was no longer "<u>his</u> Naomi Joy", but now another father's Wendy Monique. How could this be? Adam called Maggie and shared the information with her.

Maggie considered this for some time. A week later she wrote a final letter to the young lady that had been her daughter for fifteen years.

Dear "Wendy Monique",

What are dreams made of? Is it a mixture of the anticipation of joy, and the arrival of pain; the birth of hope, and the despair of disappointment? Perhaps it is where wishes and fear meet. Fact collides with fantasy. All of these, and more. Are dreams the beginning, or the end? Wendy, I have thought of this much over the past few hours—ever since I saw the ad in the classified section of the paper, under "legal notices". It told me that a young lady, previously named "Naomi Joy" would be known from now on as "Wendy Monique"...

And so, one dream dies, not with drama and flair. Oh, no. This dream dies, buried at the end of the daily news. So, the dream has both a beginning and an end.

Did I ever tell you that you were my very own "Dream Child"? What is a "Dream Child" you ask? How can I explain? Perhaps, someday, as you anticipate the arrival of your own child, you will understand.

When one is waiting, one dreams. This child will be so beautiful. She will fill this home with joy, with laughter, with a new wisdom as the world will be seen for the first time in the innocent eyes of a baby, a toddler; the first day of school for the "big, grown-up girl"! There will be shopping trips and prom dresses, mud pies and new shoes. There will be birthday cakes with beaters to lick and candles to blow out. There will be birthday wishes and Christmas surprises! There will be the very first date ~ and the worst pimple of all time on the same night! Graduation from kindergarten will give way to graduation from high school, and perhaps some day, even college. Will she be a doctor some day, or a congresswoman? Will she be happy? Someday, we might plan a wedding together—how beautiful she will be, a young woman marrying "the most wonderful man in the world"! And some day, just as I dream of holding this fresh, new and wonderful life, so I shall hold my first grandchild in my arms...

You, my beloved daughter, were such a dream, sixteen years ago ~ my Dream Child. I dreamed such dreams for you, of you, of us together. Yet, we have not been together for such a long time. I miss those dreams. How I have missed you! But, perhaps I do not miss who you have become so much as I miss who I thought you were and could be...

But, I must sound so confused. I am sorry, Wendy. I am so very confused, and sad. I wonder if putting off an old name, Naomi Joy, and putting on a new, Wendy Monique, is like taking off an old and used garment and putting on a new one, clean and radiant with the promise of many tomorrows? Is that how you feel?

Dreams die hard, Wendy. My dreams die hard. But, perhaps, the death of my dream is the beginning of yours. Wendy Monique, own your dream and go out into those promises of the tomorrows ahead of you. May they be bright and bring you fulfillment and joy. Perhaps this dream is not the end, but rather the beginning. Good bye, Wendy. We have loved you the best we knew how. May this be a new beginning for you, and may all your dreams come true.

I love you,

Mom

Epilogue

Today, I hold my grandchild in my arms. This child looks so much like you, Naomi Joy. I gaze into the tiny eyes, my finger traces the smooth cheeks and perfect lips. The tears that fall are not those of your precious baby, Naomi Joy, but my own ~ tears of joy, of wonder.

How can it be that I watched this precious life come into the world, held your hand as you gave life? Can it be true that now I hold your child in my arms? I see you in this perfect little face, my daughter. The same eyes, the same dainty ears, the same untamable hair. But there is also something different here ~ a peace, a calm, freshness…I can't really identify it, but it fills my heart with such joy…and hope.

This baby, this miracle was to carry my name! Do you remember the Scripture we taught you as a little one, Naomi Joy? The Scripture I remember when I say my middle name. Ruth ~ "I will go wherever you go and live wherever you live. Your people will be my people, and your God will be my God." Your people will be my people, and your God will be my God…It is not to be this time ~ but a baby boy is a pleasure as well! And as I see him, as I hold him, the tears that fall are tears of hope, Beloved!

Thank you, Naomi Joy. Today, I have begun to dream again…

On October 11th, 1999, Naomi Joy gave birth to her first child—a boy. This miracle also brought a miracle of healing to her heart. After countless times of being a run away, stays in jails in two different states, drug and alcohol use, and much heartache, Naomi Joy came home to us. She asked me, her adoptive mother, to be her coach as she gave birth to this very special grandchild, and I was allowed the privilege of walking her through her time of pregnancy. We witness the unfolding of a blossom that we had thought had lost its bloom many years ago. Is there hope? Can there be joy after so much pain? I wrote once that, "every joy carried with it the advent of pain."

Perhaps it is also true that pain simply increases our joy. Truly, we have exchanged beauty for ashes, the oil of joy for mourning…

The Spirit of the Lord God is upon me;
because the Lord hath anointed me
to preach good tidings unto the meek;
he hath sent me to bind up the brokenhearted,
to proclaim liberty to the captives,
and the opening of the prison to them that are bound;
To proclaim the acceptable year of the Lord,
and the day of vengeance of our God;
to comfort all that mourn;
To appoint unto them that mourn in Zion,
to give unto them beauty for ashes,
the oil of joy for mourning,
the garment of praise for the spirit of heaviness;
that they might be called
Trees of righteousness,
the planting of the Lord,
that He might be
glorified.
Isaiah 63:1-3

0-595-28188-5

Printed in the United States
45648LVS00003B/67-69

9 780595 281886